The Prosecutor

The Prosecutor

An inquiry
into the exercise of
discretion

Brian A. Grosman

University of Toronto Press

© University of Toronto Press 1969

Printed in Canada by

University of Toronto Press, Toronto and Buffalo

SBN 8020-1672-3

To my Wife

Preface

My early research into this area of the administration of criminal justice, which has remained for the most part *terra incognita*, was encouraged by Professors W. Westley, formerly chairman of the Department of Sociology, and J. J. Gow, formerly director of the Institute of Comparative and Foreign Law, both of McGill University. Throughout the period of research and writing I enjoyed the intellectual support of Dean Maxwell Cohen, and of associates and law students at the Faculty of Law. Special thanks are due to my colleague, Professor William Foster, to a former law student, Ronald Berger, to Professor J. W. Mohr of York University, Mr A. K. Gigeroff, formerly research scientist at the Clarke Institute of Psychiatry, Professor D. Morton of Osgoode-York Law School, and colleagues in the city of Toronto, who generously shared their time and advised me while I was engaged in conducting the research.

Financial assistance for the study and its publication was provided by the Foundation for Legal Research of the Canadian Bar Association and, in the initial stages, by the Institute of Comparative and Foreign Law of McGill University. Much of the writing was completed during the summer of 1968 which was spent in the peaceful village of Craftsbury Common, Vermont, among friends and neighbours who contributed the appropriate environment for production.

Particular thanks are due to those who read the manuscript and offered their helpful comments: Professor M. Friedland of the University of Toronto, Professor J. Laufer of New York State University at Buffalo, Professor M. Spector and Mr B. Smith of McGill University.

I am grateful to my secretary, Miss J. Goldsmith, who carefully typed the manuscript.

This research could not have been completed without the support of the late Henry Bull, QC, Crown Attorney of the county of York. It was his belief in the need for the continual re-evaluation of administrative practices and his generosity of spirit that made this study possible. To all those prosecutors who extended to me not only their valuable time, but kindness and warm hospitality, I owe a sincere debt of gratitude.

Faculty of Law, McGill University   B R I A N A . G R O S M A N
May 1969

Contents

The Prosecutor

CHAPTER ONE

Introduction

Very little is known about the powers exercised by prosecutors and the factors which influence their exercise of discretion. Legislative provisions which define the powers, duties, and functions of the prosecutor are significantly absent. Judicial pronouncements are, by their nature, random, restricted in scope, and for the most part directed only to the prosecutor's behaviour in the courtroom. Since the exercise of discretion is an essential element in any administrative process it might be supposed that the factors influencing the prosecutor's discretionary decisions would have been, by now, clearly established. Such, however, is not the case; agreement has been inhibited by a considerable judicial reluctance to examine the prosecutor's role beyond the formalities of his courtroom responsibilities.

The chapters that follow illustrate that it is not judicial or legislative theory which determines the prosecutor's discretion or mode of professional behaviour. Often it is the administrative demands made upon him and the informal social relationships which develop within his operational environment that control his decision-making processes. These informal factors, although crucial to any realistic appraisal of the criminal prosecuting process, have not in the past been acknowledged by legislation or by the judiciary.

There are considerable and important differences between what the prosecutor does and what the legal literature and judicial decisions say he should do. In any legal structure there is a multiplicity of aims and values. Informal adjustments are continually made in order to cope with operational realities while at the same time lip service is paid to officially stipulated means and required ends. The aim of this inquiry is to heighten the visibility of prosecutorial practices and to answer the question: Does the legal norm posit one theory of prosecutorial behaviour and actual practice reveal another? It is only when practices are revealed that we are able realistically to consider the alternatives. There is always a certain danger in attempting to reveal human activity around which crusty myths have grown up. Those who question the myths as a source of knowledge are often considered suspect. The strange insights they gain in probing the accustomed mythology pose a threat to institutional stability and customary action. Yet nothing stranger is suggested here than the affirmation of the contemporary notion that, fundamentally, law is tied to the way in which people behave. The risk involved in the advocacy of that proposition depends, not upon its empirical validity, but on the extent to which the particular myth with which this study is concerned has become enshrined in our minds.

The inquiry is focused primarily on the discretionary decision-making components of the prosecutor's role in pre-trial determinations. On one level this investigation may be likened to a comparison of a script, represented by the stated laws and their interpretation by the judiciary, with the production, the functioning realities of the system for the administration of criminal justice. On another level, by utilizing interviews which attempt to reflect faithfully the prosecutor's own conception of his role within the system, it is an inquiry into the role played by one of the key actors in the production. His reactions to the interviewer's probes have important implications for a broader attempt to understand his professional perspective and his general occupational attitudes.

Any generality about human behaviour or even the behaviour of a group of people is bound to cover up substantial heterogeneity among the individuals who make up the group. Individual values, perceptions, attitudes, and psychological characteristics are obviously different. A description of any group must be limited by the diversity of human reaction to similar situations and the incompatibility of the multi-faceted human psyche with predictable common reaction. Convergent and divergent currents which course through the membership of every social group suggest that the grouping of men according to herd characteristics or instincts or even professional conformity is gravely misdirected. Yet, at the same time, some insights into group values may be gained from an examination of persons engaged in a particular kind of work or occupational or professional enterprise.

Professional or occupational groups develop certain styles of thought. This has been illustrated by sociological studies of the police,[1] doctors,[2] dance musicians,[3] and lawyers,[4] among other occupational groups. The application of a body of specialized knowledge to attain certain specialized goals sets in some measure a group apart with collective claims upon each of its members, a certain solidarity of purpose, and even an ethos of its own. This official ethos or point of view is often reflected in group attitudes and actions.

To write about attitudes is a difficult task because the term is used in so many different senses. An attitude, for our purposes, may be defined as a combination of emotional and motivational factors which become characteristic of an individual and which is directed towards things and persons within his environment. An individual who is a member of a particular occupational or professional solidarity is likely under certain circumstances to react in certain predictable ways. In each profession men cope with problems peculiar to their occupation and their manner of coping is often reflected in their manner of thinking about and articulating their professional problems.

The empirical data for the study were drawn from interviews conducted with Crown prosecutors in one jurisdiction: the county of York which encompasses the large metropolitan city of Toronto. Before the study was begun, pilot interviews were conducted in two other metropolitan areas, Montreal and Ottawa, in order to test interview techniques, methodology, and the interview schedule.[5] These pilot studies helped to narrow the focus of the inquiry and led to the discovery of

1 W. A. Westley, "The Police: A Sociological Study of Law, Custom and Morality," 1951 (unpublished PH D thesis, University of Chicago); J. H. Skolnick, *Justice without Trial* (1966); D. J. Bordua, ed., *The Police: Six Sociological Essays* (1967).
2 Hall, "The Stages of a Medical Career," 53 *Am. J. Soc.* 327 (1948).
3 H. S. Becker, *Outsiders: Studies in the Sociology of Deviance* (1963).
4 J. E. Carlin, *Lawyers on Their Own* (1962), and *Lawyers' Ethics* (1966); Walter O. Weyrauch, *The Personality of Lawyers* (1964); Erwin O. Smigel, *The Wall Street Lawyer* (1964).
5 See Appendix I for a discussion of interview techniques and methodology and Appendix II for the interview schedule.

areas of common interest among prosecutors and certain shared perspectives which seemed capable of yielding useful data. Some forty-five prosecutors in the three cities were interviewed over an eight-month period. In addition, interviews were conducted with police officers, defence lawyers, and judges in each of these centres in order to provide background material and a variety of perspectives.

Excerpts from the interviews, found in the following chapters, were drawn from the office of the Crown Attorney in the city of Toronto where the prosecutors, twenty-five in all, were interviewed over a six-month period. There is substantial criminal activity in metropolitan Toronto and the bulk of the cases are heard by provincially appointed magistrates in Magistrates' Court in the downtown area. This is partly because of the very wide jurisdiction given to magistrates to try both indictable and non-indictable offences and also partly because most accused persons elect either to plead guilty before the magistrate or to be tried "speedily" before him.[6]

The prosecutors interviewed are members of the Bar and full-time employees of the province of Ontario. They are part of a simple administrative structure headed by the Crown Attorney who is responsible for all prosecutions under the Criminal Code for offences committed within the jurisdictional boundaries of the county of York. Although the Crown Attorney and his assistants are all nominally responsible to the provincial Attorney General, the assistant prosecutors are directly responsible for their actions to the senior prosecutor, the Crown Attorney. He in turn is responsible to the Attorney General for the conduct of the Crown Attorney's office which he heads.

Toronto was selected for the study not only because the interviewer was familiar with the criminal courts and the prosecutors in this jurisdiction, but also because the office was a highly developed administra-

---

6 In certain offences the jurisdiction of the magistrate is absolute: see s. 467 of the Criminal Code, R.S.C. 1953–4, c. 51. With the consent of the accused, the magistrate hears the vast majority of indictable offences: s. 468 of the Code. Certain offences fall within the absolute jurisdiction of the superior court of the province, namely murder, rape, political crimes such as treason, intimidating parliament, etc.: s. 413(2) of the Code, and these are the only offences over which a magistrate does not have jurisdiction either absolute or by the consent of the accused. Legislation passed after the study was completed now designates the magistrates as "Provincial Judges" and Magistrates' Courts as "Provincial Courts." An Act to Provide for Provincial Courts and Judges, R.S.O. 1968, c. 103.

tive unit. It represented one of the best examples of a well-run prosecutorial unit in Canada. Procedures and internal administrative controls had been developed over a number of years of strong administrative guidance by senior prosecutors. Haphazard procedures growing up as an answer to particular administrative demands found less encouragement than in other jurisdictions because of strong administrative and personnel supervision exercised by the Crown Attorney.

Prior to the study cautious approaches were made to gain the confidence and co-operation of the senior prosecuting officials in the area. The anticipated reluctance on the part of prosecutors to discuss difficult or problem areas of their practice did not materialize, partly because of the co-operation of the senior prosecutors, and partly because of the acceptance of the interviewer as a fellow lawyer and former prosecutor who could be expected to understand the practices and sympathize with the problems faced by those engaged in criminal prosecution.

The interviews were guided by a schedule consisting of open-ended questions.[7] Interviews were conducted in the prosecutors' offices after hours, in their homes, and often over a drink in a local tavern. The atmosphere was always one of informality and the prosecutors were encouraged to talk freely.[8] The interview excerpts are presented in the sequence in which they took place in order to avoid any suggestion

---

7 See Appendix II for the interview schedule. A closed question is so worded that it restricts the respondent's answer and is useful when the interviewer wishes the respondent to express agreement or disagreement with some stated point of view. The open question merely establishes the topic for the respondent and allows him the freedom to structure his answer as he sees fit. "The open question appears to be more appropriate when our objective is not only to discover the respondent's attitude toward some issue but also to learn something about his level of information, the structure or basis on which he has formed his opinion, the frame of reference within which he answers the question and the intensity of his feelings on the topic." R. L. Kahn and C. F. Cannell, *The Dynamics of Interviewing: Theory, Technique and Cases,* 135 (1957).

8 Carl Rogers in his two books on the subject, *Client-Centered Therapy* (1951) and *Counselling and Psycho-Therapy* (1942), first explained his "controlled non-directive probing," which was utilized as a helpful technique. Kahn and Cannell, *Dynamics,* at p. 209 suggest that "the technique of the information getting interview becomes in many ways comparable to that of the client-centered therapist. Within the topic dictated by a given content objective, the information-getting interviewer permits the respondent to communicate material at his own pace and in his own way. Like the therapist, the interviewer is permissive and accepting, regardless of the point of view or values indicated in the responses." See also R. K. Merton, M. Fiske, and P. L. Kendall, *The Focused Interview: A Manual of Problems and Procedures,* 12–13 (1956).

that they were ordered to present maximum impact or to validate certain hypotheses. Only those that reflect a pattern of response are presented. Isolated or individual responses not generally reflected in the data are not included.[9]

Any attempt to see the world through the eyes of prosecutors without making value judgments, and any effort to obtain a picture of the subject undistorted by the interviewer's own preconceptions, is fraught with difficulties.[10] There is much evidence that bias, value judgments, and other distortions relating to language and perception are unavoidable.[11] These limitations do not suggest, however, that the interview as a means of collecting information should be discarded. Although every fact received is defined by the observer's point of view, awareness of his perspective or potential bias will help to identify these limitations. This awareness is the first step towards avoiding serious distortion of the facts and the flow of communication.[12]

No doubt caution must be exercised in generalizing from data based on such a small sample and observations limited to one jurisdiction. The pre-test data from the two other jurisdictions suggest, however,

9 Although the following excerpts from the interviews may appear as isolated opinions not substantiated by concrete examples quite the contrary is the case. In most of the interviews the prosecutor pointed out his practice by examples drawn from his own experience. The inclusion of these examples would not only have added substantially to the length of the presentation, but would have created considerable problems in maintaining the anonymity of the interviewee.

10 Weyrauch, The Personality of Lawyers, at p. 9 considers the problem of the personality of the interviewer and other factors which influence the results of social research.

11 Ibid., 182, 189. For a thorough review of research dealing with interview bias, see J. J. Hyman, Interviewing for Social Research (1954). There has been considerable research in the area of psychological factors in interviewing which often illustrates that the responses obtained by interviewers tended to be related to their own opinions and reactions: see Cahalan, Tamulonius, and Verner, "Interview Bias Involved in Certain Types of Attitude Questions," 1 Intl. J. Opinion and Attitude Research 63–77 (1947); Wales, "Detection and Correction of Interviewer Bias," 16 Public Opinion Quarterly 107–22 (1952); Blankenship, "The Effect of the Interviewer upon the Response in a Public Opinion Poll," 4 J. Consulting Psychology 134–6 (1940).

Interesting studies have been conducted that deal with the effects of the interviewer's expectations rather than his opinions. See Stanton and Baker, "Interview Bias and the Recall of Incompletely Learned Materials," 5 Sociometry 123–34 (1942), where the interviews seemed to obtain results which favoured a particular response. Interviewers may suggest acceptable answers by comments on answers made by the subject. Cf. Guest, "A Study of Interviewer Competence," 1 Intl. J. Opinion and Attitude Research 17–30 (1947).

12 See H. D. Lasswell, Psychopathology and Politics, 238 (1930).

that there is a general affinity between the findings in one metropolitan area and the attitudes and practices of prosecutors in the other urban areas.

Methodology and interview technique suffer not only from the inaccuracies inherent in most social probings but, in addition, from the amateur status of the investigator. While the limitations inherent in an impressionistic, descriptive study of this kind are freely acknowledged, the remarks of a highly competent social explorer seem pertinent: "Obviously, many of these data are of doubtful worth, and my interpretations ... especially some of them ... may certainly be questionable, but I assume that a loose speculative approach to a fundamental area of conduct is better than a rigorous blindness to it."[13]

13 E. Goffman, *Behavior in Public Places*, 4 (1936).

CHAPTER TWO

An Historical
Perspective

Current prosecuting practices have been shaped by early influences common to both the Anglo-American and the French legal traditions. A brief sketch of these sources assists in placing prosecutors within an historical context and within a tradition of criminal prosecution which continues to wield a strong influence on present practices.

1 ENGLAND

By the common law of England crimes were committed not against the state but against a particular person or his family and the injured party; hence, the victim or some interested relative stepped forward in person to initiate and conduct the prosecution of the alleged offender. Since it was not the state, but private, aggrieved parties, who prosecuted, the act was carried out with a zeal that turned the law into a tool for private vengeance.

The abuses of private prosecution were acknowledged by Henry VIII who in 1534 suggested that "Those laws have been printed 'in our maternal English tongue' and are so available to all; yet they are not put into force unless it be by malice, rancour and evil will. 'Better it were that they had never been made, unless they should be put in due and perfect execution ...'"[1] To remedy the imperfect execution of the

1 T. F. T. Plucknett, quoting Henry VIII's original proposal for the draft act of 1523, in 19 *Royal Historical Society Transactions* 119, at pp. 126–7 (4th ser. 1936).

laws of the realm Henry viii proposed that the sergeants of the common weal act as police prosecutors to enforce penal statutes throughout the country.[2]

As early as 1243 the sovereign was represented by a professional attorney who prosecuted pleas of particular interest to the king.[3] These interests included, among others, proceedings against churchmen brash enough to pronounce a sentence of excommunication against a royal retainer and the investigation of certain homicides pertaining to the Crown.[4] It later developed that the king's sergeants pleaded the royal cause before the courts and the attorney general gradually took over the general supervision of the king's legal affairs. In the country at large, the public interest and crimes of no particular concern to the sovereign remained to be determined by private litigation in which the Crown generally took no interest.

From the time of Henry viii's original proposal that prosecutors be appointed throughout the country, a variety of proposals were advanced for the public prosecution of crimes by the Crown and appointed Crown officers. Some supported the public prosecution of penal infractions; others dismissed the idea in favour of a continuation of the English tradition of private prosecution. Although the king's attorneys and the king's sergeants had from the earliest times received payment from the Crown for their services, the fees gained in the private practice of law were substantially greater than those forthcoming from the Crown. It was natural, then, that the suggestion that these eminent lawyers devote themselves solely to Crown interests and forego private practice should meet some strong resistance from the incumbent Crown officers. The debate surrounding the abuses of private prosecution and the desirability of the superintendence and the conduct of criminal prosecutions by the state and state officers continued unabated throughout the nineteenth century.[5]

2 Henry viii's proposal to Parliament was unsuccessful. See G. H. Dession, *Criminal Law Administration and Public Order*, 361 n. (1948).
3 J. Ll. J. Edwards, *Law Officers of the Crown*, 15 (1964).
4 *Ibid.*, at p. 16.
5 See for the legislative history of the proposals for public prosecution, Kurland and Waters, "Public Prosecutions in England, 1854–79: An Essay in English Legislative History," 4 *Duke L. Rev.* 493 (1959). See generally, 3 Radzinowicz, *A History of English Criminal Law: The Reform of the Police* (1957).

In 1879, the office of the Director of Public Prosecutions was established and the director charged with devoting his time solely to the public service,[6] acting primarily as senior adviser to police and other prosecuting authorities.[7] At the same time it was made clear that this new and permanent prosecutorial office would not interfere with the right of any private person to institute or carry on any criminal proceeding. Today, the office of the Director of Public Prosecutions advises government departments and the police, but intervenes to conduct only those prosecutions of particular importance or difficulty including cases referred to it by government agencies and all offences formerly punishable by death.[8] In relation to the total number of prosecutions in England only a small proportion are taken by the director.[9]

The English system has remained, in principle, one of private prosecution. When the Director of Public Prosecutions or the police institute or conduct a prosecution, their status and power in law remain those of a private prosecutor. Although in theory each prosecution is private, in practice, as it has developed, individual initiative is removed from the institution and conduct of prosecutions. It is the police who most often initiate the prosecution by the laying of an information and it is they who most often prosecute cases heard in the lower courts.[10] At the higher court levels the "county" or "police" solicitor usually retains a barrister to prosecute the case on behalf of the Crown. The barrister retained is not employed by the police or by any public office, but remains aloof and independent from the investigatory procedures. He is briefed by the police solicitor as he would be by any other solicitor who might retain his services, and he therefore holds no general briefs for the Crown.[11]

6 Prosecution of Offences Act (1879), 42 & 43 Vict. c. 22.
7 See T. M. Mathew, *The Office and Duties of the Director of Public Prosecutions* (1950).
8 Regulations relating to the office are reprinted in R. M. Jackson, *The Machinery of Justice in England*, 127 (4th ed. 1964). For the evolution and recent developments in the office see Edwards, *Law Officers of the Crown*, at p. 335.
9 It is estimated that prosecution by the Director of Public Prosecutions amounts to no more than 5 per cent of the total number of prosecutions in England: Jackson, *Machinery of Justice*, at pp. 113–14.
10 *Report of the Royal Commission on the Police*, Cmnd. 1728 (1962). The commissioners criticized the practice of police acting as prosecutors in the lower courts.
11 See generally, P. Devlin, *The Criminal Prosecution in England* (1958), and P. Howard, *Criminal Justice in England* (1931).

2 UNITED STATES

Unlike the development of the public prosecution in England in the first years of the eighteenth century, most of the American colonies were doing away with private prosecutions, and as early as 1704 the first public prosecution statute was enacted: "Henceforth there shall be in every countie a sober, discreet and religious person appointed by countie courts, to be atturney for the Queen to prosecute and implead in the lawe all criminals and to doe all other things necessary or convenient as an atturney to suppresse vice and immoralitie ..."[12]

By the end of the nineteenth century official prosecutions in the majority of the newly independent United States were conducted by public prosecutors. This development, so unlike the English common law tradition of private prosecutions, was partly a product of a prevalent hostility towards all things English and a certain enthusiastic interest in French institutions. The American prosecutor, both federal and state, was patterned after both the English Attorney General and the French *avocat général* and *procureur du Roi*.[13]

By statute, in 1789, the office of the United States district attorney was created in order to "prosecute in each district all delinquents for crimes and offences cognizable under the authority of the United States."[14] At the end of the Civil War, the Attorney General of the United States was given supervisory power over all United States federal prosecutors, and his office became the law office of government known today as the Department of Justice, responsible for all federal prosecutions.

At the state level, local prosecutors called district attorneys act in their own counties much like local attorneys general with a sense of independence from state control. This may result from the elective

12 The Public Records of the Colony of Connecticut, 1636–1776, Hartford, 1850–90, 15 v. 4:468, quoted in 4 National Commission on Law Observance and Enforcement, *Report on Prosecution* (1931). See also G. R. Steinberg, "Criminal Prosecution in Connecticut," 1940 (unpublished thesis, Yale Univ. Library).

13 See the interesting treatment of the early origins of the office of the prosecutor in National Commission on Law Observance and Enforcement, *Report on Prosecution*, at pp. 7–38, where it is suggested that it was derived primarily from the French system.

14 Quoted in G. H. Dession, *Criminal Law, Administration and Public Order*, 357 (1948). Consult Dession generally for references on early development, at pp. 356–61.

nature of the office and the aggressive attitude to crime and criminals displayed in public by the incumbent in order to justify his re-election.[15] In addition to their functions as counsel in the conduct of a trial, but unlike their English counterparts, the district attorneys perform important investigatory functions concurrently with police agencies and exercise a wide discretion over the initiation of investigations, prosecutions, and the arrest of suspects. Once the information has been laid the district attorney takes over the management of the prosecution. Unlike the English system of private prosecutions and the remoteness of counsel retained for the prosecution from the investigatory and initiatory charging processes of the police, the American prosecutor combines the functions of police adviser with those of prosecutor at the trial. The federal prosecuting system in the United States very much resembles the French structure, and yet at the local level in each state the independence of the prosecutor and his freedom from supervisory control is a unique development born of the hardy independence of a young country disenchanted with past attempts at forced centralization.[16]

3 FRANCE

The early development of criminal prosecutions in France closely resembled that in England. Until the thirteenth century all criminal proceedings in France were governed by the maxim, "In France, no one pleads by procurator save the King." Criminal actions were purely private litigations and it was not considered lawful for anyone to bring an accusation except in his own name, or for his family, or for his liege

15 In 1931 the "Wickersham Committee" investigating the administration of Criminal justice in the United States was critical of the elective nature of the prosecutor's office and the resulting close connection between the office and politics. Cf. National Commission on Law Observance and Enforcement, *Report on Prosecution*, at pp. 14–15. In all but five states prosecutors are elected.
16 For an excellent series of articles dealing with the development and duties of American district attorneys see Baker and De Long, "The Prosecuting Attorney: Provisions of Law Organizing the Office," 23 *J. Crim. L. C. & P.S.* 926 (1932–3); Baker, "The Prosecutor-Initiation of Prosecution," 23 *J. Crim. L. C. & P.S.* 770 (1932–3); Baker and De Long, "The Prosecuting Attorney: Powers and Duties in Criminal Prosecution," 24 *J. Crim. L. C. & P.S.* 1025 (1933–4); R. Moley, *Politics and Criminal Prosecution* (1929); and the recent report of the President's Commission on Law Enforcement and Administration of Justice, *Task Force Report: The Courts* (1967).

lord.[17] When the interests of the king or his nobles were at stake the right *demander par procureur* prevailed. Initially these procureurs were practising lawyers who, as part of their private practice, would superintend the king's fiscal interests as well as prosecute certain offences punishable by fines and forfeitures which were one of the chief sources of revenue for the king and his nobles.[18] By the fourteenth century the position of *procureur du roi* was firmly entrenched, establishing the predominance of *l'action publique,* and paving the way for the rising importance of the *ministère public.*[19]

The French historical development is marked by four successive modes of prosecution: *l'accusation privée, l'accusation populaire, la poursuite d'office,* and *l'accusation publique.*[20] Originally, the victim or his heirs instituted proceedings for reasons of self-interest. *L'accusation populaire,* which followed later, was characterized as a private action taken in the interest of the state. This was superseded by *la poursuite d'office* whereby the judge himself would, in the public interest, assume the role of *accusateur* for serious crimes. The last and present mode of prosecution is *l'accusation publique,* by which state-appointed officials are charged with the investigation, preparation, and prosecution of all criminal cases. The *procureur public* and his assistants represent the Minister of Justice and function as a unit (*parquet*) at each court level. The Minister of Justice ranks first in the prosecuting hierarchy, followed by the *avocat général,* attached to the *Cour de Cassation;* the *procureurs généraux,* attached to the Court of Appeal; and the *procureurs de la République* and their assistants.

The *procureur de la République,* who is assigned to a court of primary jurisdiction, is to "undertake, or cause to be undertaken, all action necessary to discover and prosecute breeches of the penal law."[21] He is

17 See A. Esmein, *The History of Continental Criminal Procedures* (1913); H. Regnault, *Manuel d'histoire de droit français* (1947).
18 P. C. Timbal, *Histoire des institutions publiques et des faits sociaux,* 403 (1961).
19 See R. Gerraud, 1 *Traité théorique et practique d'instruction criminelle et de procédure pénale,* 162 (1907). See also Ploscowe, "Development of Inquisitorial and Accusatorial Elements in French Procedure," 23 *J. Crim. L. C. & P.S.* 372 (1932–3); Tyndale, "Organization and Administration of Justice in France," 8 *Can. Bar Rev.* 567 (1930), and Tyndale, "Organization and Administration of Justice in France," 9 *Can. Bar Rev.* 655 (1931).
20 Garraud, *Traité théorique,* at pp. 162–3.
21 Article 41, French Code of Criminal Procedure, as translated by G. L. Kock in 7 *American Series of Foreign Penal Codes* (1964).

thereby empowered to receive complaints and has the right to require police assistance in the performance of his duties. It is the *procureur de la République* who is responsible for initiating the prosecutions and who also supervises the officers of the judicial police in their investigations.[22]

The similarities between the *procureur de la République* and the local district attorney in the United States are primarily related to the scope of their functions. Both act not only to control the conduct of the trial as professional prosecutors, but also to initiate prosecutions and to supervise police investigation. It is in the career patterns of the two that the dissimilarity is most patent: the one is a public official in a rigidly structured civil service hierarchy, the other acts as an elected political figure with wide discretion and freedom of action.

4 CANADA

In Canada, the Crown officers were originally located at the seat of government and prosecutions were conducted at this central locale. As the population expanded into areas more remote from the central authority, the Attorney General and his agents, the law officers of the Crown, could not effectively attend to their duties.[23] By 1857 a county attorney was appointed by the Governor-in-Council for every county in Upper Canada.[24] These were local lawyers who acted as part-time prosecutors appointed and generally supervised by the Attorney General. Local county attorneys became responsible not only for the prosecution of crimes in their respective counties, but often acted to supervise the administration of criminal justice in their locality.

With Confederation in 1867, criminal law and procedure was designated by the British North America Act as being within federal competence.[25] The Attorney General of Canada was to regulate, conduct, and defend all criminal proceedings for the Crown or any federal department with respect to any subject matter, apart from the Criminal

22 *Ibid.*, art. 42.
23 Bull, "The Crown Attorney's Office," *Obiter Dicta*, Spring 1954, at p. 39; and Bull, "The Career Prosecutor in Canada," 53 *J. Crim. L. C. & P.S.* 91 (1962).
24 An Act Respecting the Appointment of Local Crown Attorneys, 20 Vict. 59 (Can.), reported in the Consolidated Statutes for Upper Canada (1859).
25 British North America Act (1867), 30 & 31 Vict. c. 3, s. 91(27) (Imp.).

Code, and within the legislative jurisdiction of the federal government. The provinces through their own Attorneys General assumed responsibility for the constitution of the criminal courts and the administration of criminal justice. Their jurisdiction included the regulation of provincial courts and law enforcement within the province as well as the prosecution of provincial and criminal code offences and the appointment of local Crown prosecutors and magistrates.[26]

Private prosecutions and those brought by municipal and federal government departments are conducted by specially retained lawyers.[27] The prosecutor specially retained by a federal government department to prosecute locally generally remains remote from the investigatory and charging procedures and prosecution, based as it is on individual case retainers, resembles English practice.[28] Federal prosecutions represent only a small portion of the criminal prosecutions in Canada. But even in these the provincial Attorney General, through his provincially appointed Crown prosecutor, may intervene where in the interests of justice he deems it appropriate to do so.[29]

In Canada there has been a tradition of part-time Crown prosecutors, often lawyers appointed as a result of political patronage who, in addition to their private practice of law, assume prosecuting duties. The employment of part-time prosecutors has become untenable in the face of growing urban crime and the resulting administrative demands. Familiarity with the system and a certain expertise is coming to be expected from the Crown prosecutor. It is now generally accepted that only with a permanent Crown prosecutor and a permanent Crown prosecuting structure can these new demands be adequately answered in urban areas.

It was the local Crown Attorney or prosecutor appointed by the provincial Attorney General who conducted and continues to conduct

26 See 2 Ontario Royal Commission Inquiry into Civil Rights, *Report no. 1* at pp. 936–47 (1968), for an account of the functions and duties of the Attorney General of the province of Ontario.
27 See Kaufman, "The Role of the Private Prosecutor," 7 *McGill L. J.* 102 (1960).
28 Federal government departments retain lawyers to act as local agents for prosecutions under federal legislation such as Narcotic Control Act, Food and Drugs Act, etc. Recently permanent federal prosecutors have been assigned to Montreal and Toronto; they now conduct all federal prosecutions in those jurisdictions and are directly responsible to the Minister of Justice as officers of the federal Department of Justice.
29 Crown Attorney's Act, R.S.O. 1960, c. 82, s. 14.

the great bulk of the prosecutions throughout the counties. Every local Crown prosecutor is an agent of the provincial Attorney General for the purpose of prosecutions under the provisions of the Criminal Code and provincial statutes. Today, in the larger metropolitan areas, the permanent Crown prosecutor is usually a full-time salaried Crown officer. He is prohibited from engaging in private practice and must devote his time to the duties of his office. He takes no part in civil litigation on behalf of the province or municipality. In rural areas he is often a local lawyer carrying on a private practice, appointed as Crown agent for prosecutions in his county and paid by the province on a fee basis. In summary conviction and other minor criminal prosecutions a police officer may appear as agent of the provincial Attorney General to conduct the proceedings, although this practice is generally frowned upon.[30]

The permanent Crown prosecutor is a public officer and a provincial civil servant responsible to the Attorney General of the province. Although the latter may prefer to appoint members from the ranks of his own political party the full-time Crown prosecutor, once appointed, does not engage in overt political activity. Changes in the government of the day do not affect his tenure as he has become, in the larger urban centres, more a civil servant than a political appointee.

The prosecutor in Canada has come to resemble more his French, Scottish,[31] or American counterpart than his English confederate. But, unlike the American district attorney, once appointed he is non-political and plays little part in initiating criminal prosecutions or in supervising and directing police investigation. Unlike the French *procureur de la République*, the Canadian Crown prosecutor has not been specifically groomed for his duties, but is a lawyer educated as other lawyers. It is expected that he will develop the necessary expertise once he begins prosecuting.

---

30 See *supra*, at p. 12, n. 10, and the recent case of *R. v. Campbell and Pool, ex parte MacLeod*, [1967] 1 c.c.c. 168. For a comment on the propriety of provincial police, magistrates' and prosecutors' responsibility to, and supervision by, the same authority, the provincial Attorney General, see Edwards, "Penal Reform and the Machinery of Justice in Canada," 8 *Crim. L.Q.* 421 (1966).

31 The Canadian system of full-time provincial prosecutors responsible to the Attorney General of the province resembles, and may have been influenced, by the Scottish system where prosecutions are conducted by procurators-fiscal working under the supervision of the Lord Advocate.

In urban areas today the large bulk of prosecutions is conducted by a permanent professional prosecutor who represents the Crown with a considerable freedom of action.[32] The independence of the prosecutor from the police, and the initiating and investigatory procedures in accord with the traditional concept associated with the English barrister, have been modified by Canadian practice. The Canadian prosecutor often acts not only as an advocate for the Crown at the trial; in addition, his contacts with the police are more substantial than those of his counterpart in England, but are far from reaching the state of interdependence of police and prosecution that prevails in the United States.

32 An exception to this practice is that current in British Columbia. Organized municipalities are responsible for their own administration of justice. Accordingly, prosecutors are appointed and paid by the municipality and in some, such as Vancouver, are full-time appointees, while in smaller communities are part-time and may even be appointed on an *ad hoc* basis. In unorganized territory prosecutors are appointed by the provincial Attorney General on an *ad hoc* basis, as they are for all trials in the superior courts of criminal jurisdiction.

CHAPTER THREE

Initiating the
Prosecution

1 THE DECISION TO ARREST

Although empowered to initiate criminal proceedings by complaint or information, in practice the prosecutor rarely participates in the charging stage and does not assume responsibility for prosecution until after the charge has been laid.[1] Individuals, whether private citizens or police officers, commence criminal proceedings by information or complaint sworn before a justice of the peace. The prosecutor's first duty is to examine the charge or information in order to make the decision whether to prosecute or not. In this way he performs a screening function by reviewing the sufficiency of the evidence before initiating the prosecution. The exercise of an independent judgment, in addition to the police decision to arrest, provides some protection against the institution of unwarranted prosecutions or those based on insufficient evidence.

A study of prosecutions in the county of York indicates that in the majority of cases prosecutors do not in fact consider the information or the charge until after the accused is arraigned before the court. The sufficiency of the evidence against the accused often is not reviewed until the preliminary hearing or the trial itself is reached.[2] The decision,

---

1 C.C. S. 439 provides that "anyone" may lay an information. A Crown Attorney seems to be embraced by the term "anyone." See, for example, *Re Anthony* (1932), 5 M.P.R. 498, 59 C.C.C. 158 (N.S.C.A.).
2 In federal prosecutions under the Narcotic Control Act, R.S.C. 1960–1, C. 35, counsel retained to prosecute as a rule will review police evidence prior to the laying of charges.

then, to institute a prosecution is made by the arresting officer when he decides that there is sufficient evidence of the commission of an offence to justify an arrest. Thus, police decisions to arrest constitute the effective decision to initiate prosecution, although the standards justifying an arrest may differ substantially from the standards of evidence required to justify the institution of a prosecution.[3]

The prosecutor will rarely be informed about the facts of the case before the accused has been charged and is arraigned in court. At the arraignment it is customary for a police liaison officer to pass the "dope sheet" to the prosecutor. In that fleeting moment, between the calling of the case and the moment when the prosecutor reaches his feet, he reviews the dope sheet which contains a brief police summary of the evidence against the accused. Inadequacies in the charge or the evidence are seldom reviewed by the prosecutor at this first arraignment. After arraignment, inadequacies will usually continue unnoticed and un-remedied until the preliminary hearing is held. The accused may plead guilty or waive the preliminary hearing. If the former, problems of proof and the adequacies of the charges will not be reviewed; if the latter, review will be delayed until the prosecutor prepares the case for trial.

The prosecutors in the county of York acknowledge their lack of control over the laying of charges and the problems inherent in delayed prosecutorial participation. Since the vast majority of charges are laid by police officers without any prior consultation with prosecuting authorities, inconsistencies between probable cause for arrest and sufficiency of proof for purposes of prosecution go completely unnoticed. One prosecutor responded to the situation as follows: "I don't know what I have on from day to day. I enjoy the challenge of walking in cold and looking at the dope sheets." Another pointed out that his first

3 The standards required for an arrest, i.e., "reasonable and probable grounds," may not correspond with the standards of evidence required to institute a prosecution. In Canada we equate the two. LaFave has concluded: "While the arrest decision quite clearly sets the outer limits of law enforcement, it does not in the usual case set the actual limits of prosecution. The separate and distinct decision on whether to prosecute, ordinarily made by the prosecutor (u.s.), serves both as a safeguard to insure that individuals are not prosecuted when adequate evidence is lacking or when sound policy reasons dictate to the contrary and also as a screen against the system becoming clogged with insignificant cases." W. R. LaFave, *Arrest: The Decision to Take a Suspect into Custody*, 58 (1965).

contact with the case begins "... usually the day I walk into court. The day the case comes up for the first time is the first time I see it. In the major part of the cases I do not even see the police first ..." A third voiced some concern over the delayed timing of his participation:

Ninety-five per cent of the time we come in post charge. The other five per cent of the time an opinion may be asked by an officer as to what sort of charge he should lay. This doesn't happen nearly enough. If our advice is sought we'd knock a lot of things out, right off the bat. These things later take up the time of the courts and end up in acquittals. If the right charge had been laid at the beginning we would avoid a lot of problems later. Out of four hundred cases there are only one or two where the police would have been advised as to the laying of the charge. In the majority of the cases we get introduced to the case the morning of the trial. In magistrates' court, we first get instructions in the matter the morning that the case is coming up in court, possibly for a remand. We have little control over the laying of charges.

Still another suggested that some of the negative aspects of the late scrutiny by the prosecution of police charging decisions could be avoided: "If the police get into the habit of speaking to the prosecutor we can sometimes avoid laying charges which we cannot prove." The limitations of time available at the arraignment to review adequately the sufficiency of the charges was illustrated by a prosecutor who said, "The only screening of the police charges is if they ask you for your advice. Or you may pick up the dope sheet and see the wrong charge and may advise the police to lay a different information. But it is rare – because of the speed of the remands in the cases in magistrates' court you don't have much time to catch that."

The emotional involvement of the police in a criminal prosecution is not conducive to a disinterested or independent judgment whether or not a prosecution is warranted by the facts. The decision whether or not to invoke the criminal process against a person is best made by a prosecutor trained in the law rather than by the police decision to arrest. If charges laid by the police were screened by a prosecutor in order to assess the sufficiency of the evidence available and the likelihood of a conviction on that charge, the court case load could be substantially decreased and the number of successful prosecutions would increase proportionately with the effectiveness of the screening process; for only those cases would proceed where, in the judgment of the prosecutor, the evidence was sufficient in law to support a conviction for the offence charged. Institution of adequate pre-arraignment screening procedures ultimately would substantially increase the number of guilty pleas entered and discourage frivolous defences.

It could be argued that participation by the prosecutor at these early pre-charging stages is inappropriate, for it is just that remoteness, encouraged by the prosecutor's practice of *not* supervising police decisions to prosecute, that insures his impartiality at trial. If, in screening charges, the prosecutor renders the decision to prosecute after reviewing the evidence, he might become a convinced advocate committed to conviction, and prosecute with partiality in order to prove that his original assessment was correct.

Pre-arraignment case assessment by a lawyer, not engaged in prosecutions, would safeguard the independence of the screening judgment.

2 POLICE DISCRETION

In the vast majority of cases, then, the decision whether or not to invoke the criminal process is one which is made by the arresting officer and not the prosecutor. Under these circumstances, the criminal process may or may not be initiated against a person guilty of criminal conduct for reasons peculiar to the individual police officer. His exercise of discretion may be based on individual attitudes toward the accused, the nature of his offence or upon the internal policies of the local enforcement authorities. Decisions to initiate or not to initiate criminal proceedings are made by the police for individual or policy reasons which are not officially visible and are not always subject to judicial supervision or legislative control.[4] The police and the prosecutor may disagree on the criteria on which decisions not to invoke the criminal process should be based. The prosecutor may best be equipped to make

4 See Goldstein, "Police Discretion Not to Invoke the Criminal Process: Low-Visibility Decisions in the Administration of Justice," 69 *Yale L.J.* 543 (1960), and LaFave, *Arrest,* at pp. 67–143, where the police decision not to invoke the criminal process and the criteria on which the decision is often based are discussed in some detail.

the policy decision involved but, because of his limited participation in the pre-arraignment process, these decisions are in practice made by the police prior to prosecutorial contact with the case.

However, once the accused has been brought before the court the prosecutor may exercise his discretion not to proceed by withdrawing the charges. By this stage in the proceedings the accused has been subjected to the stigmatizing effect of arrest, criminal charge, pre-trial detention, and arraignment in a criminal court. Human and financial resources have been expended in the defence of what are often unwarranted prosecutions. The accused is subjected to the serious impositions of a criminal prosecution, the expense of his defence, and the disruption of his life and status in the community which criminal prosecution inevitably entails.

In a few cases the prosecutor is consulted by the police prior to the laying of the charge. These consultations are limited to charges involving major crimes such as murder or complicated business frauds and bankruptcies where charges must be carefully framed, or in cases that have or may gain substantial public notoriety. A senior prosecutor outlined the limits of pre-charge consultation:

In the big complicated frauds you're consulted prior to arrest and also you're consulted more often as you get older because as you are more senior in the Crown office, you're in your office more often, and you're available more often because you're not in magistrate's courts all day. In a complicated business fraud we might be asked to draft the charge, or when it is an offence that is rarely used. For example, a lumber company was selling lumber graded higher than the quality of the lumber permitted. I was consulted and laid a charge in regard to selling lumber with a counterfeit stamp on it. Similarly, a man sent poisoned chocolate candies to his neighbours. In that case I also drafted the charge. These are cases that are out of the ordinary. In most cases, if the police are the informants they draft the charge and the justice of the peace swears it. If it's a private complaint, the charge is drafted by an employee of the magistrates' court office.

Another prosecutor said:

The police may scoop him on a general count of fraud and then consult you in regard to specific charges and the evidence required. But once the charge is laid, the police have no control ... It is only when you get a complicated case or when a certain amount of diplomacy is required because a big name is involved that the police may call you before they nail him. There is no control really until after the charge is laid. Then you can tell them to get further evidence if you think the case is weak. But you really have no control until the charge is laid.

Generally, prosecutorial advice at the pre-charge stage is conditional on the police decision to seek the advice. This is done only in non-routine cases, those which pose difficult questions of fact or law. For example, proposed prosecutions for the publication and distribution of obscene literature will usually depend on the opinion of the prosecutor. Once the prosecutor has determined that the materials are obscene, in the light of current judicial standards, the arrest and prosecution will be instituted. Unlike other prosecutors, a prosecutor designated to deal with complicated business frauds and bankruptcy acts as an adviser to the police on questions relating to the nature of the evidence required and the drafting of charges. But cases of a prosecutor's pre-charge participation, either by designation or by chance police request, represent less than five per cent of the total prosecuted; in the remaining cases his participation begins in the courtroom and not before.

Most prosecutors draw a clear distinction between the investigatory function, which they believe is clearly a police function, and the prosecutorial function, which commences only after the police investigation is complete and the charge has been laid. It is made clear from the interviews that the prosecutor does not lay charges nor does he institute proceedings.[5] "I get knowledge about the accused from the police and I rarely come into the case prior to the laying of a charge. If the police want advice it's usually an unusual case and I don't suggest that charges be laid. A prosecutor doesn't complain and you don't institute proceedings." A senior prosecutor stated clearly:

I'm not going to direct their investigation of the accused or the witnesses. I have no more right to direct police techniques than they have to direct my trial techniques. I express my opinion to them. It does not happen too much in regard to advising them prior to arrest because they have trained senior officers now who can make as valid a decision as I can. In rural areas you would be called on more often.

5 See Bull, "The Career Prosecutor in Canada," 53 *J. Crim. L. & P.S.* 89, at p. 94 (1962). "He does not in practice institute criminal proceedings on his own initiative."

3 FRAGMENTATION OF CROWN RESPONSIBILITY

During the progress of a case from the first arraignment to the trial, different prosecutors appear at each of the stages of the case up to and including the trial. One prosecutor may appear at the original arraignment of the accused, a second on the application for bail, a third on the second arraignment, a fourth at the preliminary hearing, and, finally, a fifth prosecutor may conduct the trial. This "balkanization" of Crown responsibility perpetuates original errors caused by the inadequate screening of charges and evidence. No one prosecutor is given, or assumes, responsibility for the conduct of a case from the first arraignment through to trial. As a result, it is often only when the case has reached the trial itself that the prosecutor assigned to the trial will review and prepare the prosecution's case. It is at this late stage that he may become aware of the limitations of the evidence or the inadequacy of the charge.

In the county of York, prosecutors are not assigned cases but rather courtrooms so that a single prosecutor is seldom given responsibility for the conduct of a case from the first arraignment through to trial. The newer appointees are made responsible for one of the lower courts (the magistrates' courts), their more experienced colleagues conduct the trials by judge alone and by judge and jury in the sessions courts, and the most experienced conduct the murder, rape, and complicated fraud and bankruptcy cases which are heard in the superior court of criminal jurisdiction. Only in the latter cases, tried for the most part by a superior court judge and jury, will a prosecutor assume responsibility for the case from the first arraignment to its eventual disposition. One of the senior prosecutors confirmed that it is only senior or experienced men who are assigned to cases rather than to courtrooms: "The point of time of contact with a case depends on the level at which a prosecutor is prosecuting. At my present level, in many cases, I will take the preliminary hearing and take the case right through until trial, whereas a young prosecutor might first see the case just before it was to come up in magistrates' court."

Case assignments are rare and probably make up no more than two or three per cent of the total number of cases prosecuted. For even in a rape case, which must proceed to a superior court to be tried by a judge and jury, it is common practice that three or four different prosecutors will have participated as the case progresses through the stages to its ultimate disposition in the superior court. Costly errors are discovered belatedly because of the combination of the lack of scrutiny and fragmented responsibility. All the prosecutors interviewed seemed aware of these problems. One said simply, "It would be ideal if one man could follow it through from beginning to end."

The burdens of the prosecutors' case load limit individual case assignments. The adequacy of the charge and evidence against the accused is not seriously weighed until it is absolutely necessary to do so. The original charging decision may have been made by a police officer in the heat of an emergency where he may have had little time for reflection. Similarly the overburdened lower court docket leaves little time for reflection by prosecutors on the sufficiency of the charge in each case which comes before the court. Thus it seldom happens that the police arrest a person whom the prosecutor refuses to charge or against whom the prosecution refuses to proceed. It is only in the later stages of the process, during the preliminary or grand jury hearing, or at the trial itself, that there is time for reflection on the sufficiency of the original charges and the proof against the accused.

4 INADEQUATE REVIEW OF EVIDENCE

In effect great confidence is placed by the prosecuting authorities in the competency of the police officer on the beat, for his decision to arrest is adopted as their decision to prosecute. Thus, the question of who then makes the decision to prosecute and what are the criteria on which that decision is based, can only be answered in terms of police arrest and charge policies, and the individual officer's decision that probable cause exists to effect an arrest. In other words, police discretion dominates the initiation of criminal prosecution. The exercise of this judgment becomes more important when it is recalled that, except for the few complicated cases, the arraignment represents the prosecutor's first contact with the case. The dominance over the whole invocation of criminal prosecution of the original decision to arrest and of the police standards for arrests may seriously impair the actual independence of the prosecutor from police enforcement policies and the effective limits of his prosecuting function.

If the accused enters a plea of guilty the police decision is never reviewed. If, on the other hand, a plea of not guilty is entered, do the institutional controls serve as an effective screening process to test the sufficiency of the police decision to arrest, which has become the basis for invoking a criminal prosecution? The preliminary hearing, if not waived by the accused, may act as a check upon the charging decision of the police. Magistrates, however, in turn rely on the judgment of the police and the prosecution, and are reluctant to intervene at this early stage to dismiss a prosecution unless the lack of evidence is patent. As a result, co-operative, non-interventionist attitudes adhered to by both the prosecutor and the magistrate support the original police decision. If the accused is represented by defence counsel, gross evidentiary deficiences may be pointed out. But if he remains unrepresented, the prosecution may easily establish a *prima facie* case against the accused without a probing of its sufficiency.

The apparent rigour of the extension of the police decision to arrest and its *de facto* adoption as the standard for initiating prosecutions, although seemingly pervasive, is mitigated by current pre-trial practices which encourage flexibility of alternatives. The police decision to charge may be reviewed before trial if the prosecutor believes that pre-trial alternatives may expedite the disposition of the case by the entry of a guilty plea. A variety of considerations may be explored by prosecution and defence at this early stage. This exploration anticipates the exercise of prosecutorial discretion to reconsider the sufficiency of the charge in the light of defence proposals and the likelihood of the entry of a guilty plea. Discretion exercised in a multitude of ways by the prosecution before trial may subject police decisions to charge to prosecutorial scrutiny which is otherwise seemingly absent.

CHAPTER FOUR

Discretion and
Pre-trial Practices

1 THE GUILTY PLEA

Adversarial disputes attract prime judicial attention although the majority of criminal convictions are based on the acceptance by the court of a plea of guilty entered by the accused. The plea of guilty to the charge is entered in open court and is subject to the limited judicial inquiry whether the accused understands the nature of the charge and whether the plea is voluntary. The accused's affirmative reply ends the inquiry and the plea is accepted. If the court suspects that the accused is confused and does not understand the nature of the charge, or if the charges are technical and the accused is youthful or of limited intelligence, the judge may attempt to clarify a charge for the accused in order to ascertain that it is clearly understood. A plea of guilty is equivalent to an admission by the accused that the prosecution could, if necessary, establish his guilt in fact and in law.[1] Consequently, when it appears that the plea may have been involuntary, or when it is or may have been the result of inducements held out by a person in authority, the court will, under these circumstances, conduct an inquiry into the basis for the plea.[2] There is little judicial interest in conducting any further inquiry into the factual basis of the plea or the motivations of the accused in making the plea or the prosecution in accepting it. The court relies on the prosecutor's judgment when accepting a plea of

1 R. v. Roop, 57 N.S.R. 325, 42 C.C.C. 344, [1924] 3 D.L.R. 985. See also R. v. Inglis (1917), 23 Argus L.R. 378 (Aust.).
2 Guerin v. R. (1933), 55 Que. K.B. 84, 60 C.C.C. 350 (C.A.) per Walsh J. referring to R. v. Brown (1848), 17 L.J.M.C. 145; and R. v. Dawson (1924), 18 Cr. App. R. 111. See the recent case of Brosseau v. R., [1969] 3 C.C.C. 129.

guilty; if the plea is acceptable to the prosecution it is acceptable to the court. There is little judicial interest in inquiring whether the accused's plea is the result of prior discussions between the prosecution and the defence or the police and the defence, or whether it is a result of the accused's expectation that he will achieve greater leniency by his plea of guilty than he could expect at trial.[3]

A court may act on the assumption that the entry of a guilty plea is a sign of remorse indicative of the accused's interest in rehabilitation. This acceptance suggests a naïveté or unawareness that insulates some judges from the realities of the pre-trial market place. Entry of a plea of guilty often is the result of astute pre-trial negotiations by defence counsel or of the accused's own manipulation of the pre-trial alternatives. His willingness to engage in negotiations before entering a guilty plea for concessions, such as a reduction of the charge or charges, reflects not so much repentance as it does the accused's desire to obtain the best result with the least risk.

The recent report in the United States of the President's Commission on Law Enforcement and the Administration of Criminal Justice recognized the pervasive influence of "plea-bargaining": "In form, a plea-bargain can be anything from a series of careful conferences to a hurried consultation in a courthouse corridor. In content it can be anything from a conscientious exploration of the facts and dispositional alternatives available and appropriate to a defendant, to a perfunctory deal ..."[4]

It is this series of pre-trial negotiations which often provide the impetus for prosecutorial screening of police decisions to charge. They do so by encouraging an evaluation of the strength and weaknesses of the prosecution's case, and the exploration of alternatives available. These steps are taken to facilitate disposition without entering into the formal trial process. Post-arraignment screening of charges during negotiations serves administrative purposes and makes available to the prosecution, in exchange for a plea of guilty, alternatives which would be unavailable if pre-arraignment screening were made effective.

---

3 The reluctance of the court to inquire behind the plea of guilty was recently demonstrated in the case of R. v. Behr, [1967] 3 C.C.C. 1. This decision was subsequently reversed by the Ontario Court of Appeal which permitted the entry of a plea of not guilty and ordered a new trial, [1968] 2 C.C.C. 151.

4 The Challenge of Crime in a Free Society: A Report by the President's Commission on Law Enforcement and the Administration of Justice, 11 (1967).

2 THE TWILIGHT ZONE

The compromise of charges in return for the entry of a guilty plea is theoretically without sanction and accordingly takes place without court scrutiny or control. The propriety of the prosecutor's exercise of discretionary power during pre-trial proceedings has been the subject of much debate.[5] Although little has been written on the Canadian experience, the American literature indicates that prosecutors in the United States do exercise a broad discretion in deciding whether to prosecute offenders, and whether to enforce certain laws. Dean Roscoe Pound suggested that discretion is "an authority conferred by law to act in certain conditions or situations in accordance with an official's or an official agency's own considered judgment and conscience. It is an idea of morals belonging to the twilight zone between law and morals."[6]

It has been said that "the discretionary power exercised by the prosecuting attorney in initiation, accusation, and discontinuing prosecution, gives him more control over an individual's liberty and reputation than any other public official."[7] The decision to initiate the prosecution is, in many jurisdictions in the United States, one of the prosecutor's primary responsibilities. He exercises his discretion by the selection of those cases which he feels should be prosecuted and the rejection of those which he feels should not.[8] Despite statutory provisions, there

5 W. R. LaFave, *Arrest: The Decision to Take a Suspect into Custody*, at p. 9, points out that the exercise of discretion is common to all stages in the administration of criminal justice, but is recognized as proper only at the post-conviction stages. See generally, Brietel, "Controls in Criminal Law Enforcement," 27 *U. of Chi. L. Rev.* 427 (1960); R. Moley, *Politics and Criminal Prosecution* 74–9 (1929); Arnold, "Law Enforcement: An Attempt at Social Dissection," 42 *Yale L.J.* 1, at p. 18 (1932).
6 Pound, "Discretion, Dispensation and Mitigation: The Problem of the Individual Special Case," 35 *N.Y.U.L. Rev.* 925, at p. 926 (1960).
7 Note, "Prosecutor's Discretion," 103 *U. of Pa. L. Rev.* 1057 (1954–5). See Hobbs, "Prosecutor's Bias: An Occupational Disease," 2 *Ala. L. Rev.* 40, at p. 41 (1949); Jackson, "The Federal Prosecutor," 31 *J. of Crim. L. & C.* 3 (1940); Baker and De Long, "The Prosecuting Attorney and his Office," 25 *J. Crim. L. C. & P.S.* 695, at p. 719 (1935).
8 See Baker and De Long, "The Prosecuting Attorney: Powers and Duties in Criminal Prosecution," 24 *J. Crim. L. C. & P.S.* 1025, at p. 1064 (1933–4); Baker, "The Prosecutor: Initiation of Prosecution," 23 *J. Crim. L. C. & P.S.* 770 (1932–3); Klein, "District Attorney's Discretion Not to Prosecute," 32 *L.A.B. Bull.* 323 (1957). LaFave suggests that the police seek a warrant when they desire the advice of the prosecutor before arrest. He concludes (*Arrest*, at p. 46): "In these

appears to be little state control over the freedom of local district attorneys to make these determinations.[9] Debate in the United States has centred on the question whether it would be desirable to impose limitations on the exercise of prosecutorial discretion.[10]

In Canada, we have yet to ask the crucial questions in order to discover under what conditions or situations discretion is exercised. Under what circumstances will the prosecution enter into plea negotiations, either to reduce charges from the more serious to the less serious or included offence, or to reduce the number of charges outstanding against the accused? What are the benefits that accrue to the prosecution from engaging in plea negotiations? What are the reasons for its current use in pre-trial practice?

Unlike civil actions, where conciliation and compromise are judicially accepted and encouraged, in criminal prosecutions a man is either guilty or innocent of the crime with which he is charged. He cannot be somewhat guilty or somewhat innocent. If the charge cannot be proven he is freed; if it can be proven he is convicted. In theory, criminal cases cannot be settled. The following comments by a senior prosecutor illustrate the continuing dichotomy between the theory and practice:

There is no doubt that criminal cases do get settled. It goes on all the time. If we fought out every case on our list we'd be twenty thousand cases behind. As the case load gets higher and higher there is more and more pressure to settle cases. In the magistrates' court, I'd say that twenty per cent are settled. We'd be willing to settle more of them, but defence counsel are unable to convince their clients to plead guilty to anything. As you get higher it would be about the same. In the Supreme Court assizes there were sixteen

cases the prosecutor quite clearly makes a decision to prosecute when he approves the warrant." Snyder, "The District Attorney's Hardest Task," 30 J. Crim. L. C. & P.S. 167 (1939) at p. 173 suggests that it is the prosecutor's primary duty to select only the strategic cases for prosecution: "... the best of district attorneys must still winnow his cases in order to select only the strategic, if his efforts are to be successful in any measurable degree ... [otherwise] ... he would create an adverse public clamor about *persecuting* so many cases instead of *prosecuting* the right ones."

9 Ploscowe, "The Significance of Recent Investigations for the Criminal Law and Administration of Criminal Justice," 100 U. of Pa. L. Rev. 805, at p. 824 (1952); See "Report of the A.B.A. Commission on Organized Crime," 76 A.B.A. Rep. 385, at p. 402 (1951).

10 "Plea-bargaining" has been criticized as unethical and contrary to Anglo-American notions of criminal justice. Cf. Arnold, "Law Enforcement: An Attempt at Social Dissection," 42 Yale L.J. 1, at p. 18 (1932); Breitel, "Controls in Criminal Law Enforcement," 27 U. of Chi. L. Rev. 427 (1960).

or seventeen cases. One was a pretty good case of capital murder but there were pitfalls in the case for the Crown witnesses and the two accused had been drinking. The prosecution accepted a plea to non-capital murder. The prosecution was delighted and the accused were delighted. There was also a rape case. It was a crummy case and the defence lawyer could probably have walked away with nothing but somebody told him to plead guilty to indecent assault and he did that. There was also a criminal negligence case which looked barely like dangerous driving. The defence was happy to get rid of the criminal negligence and wanted to plead to dangerous driving and I was delighted to accept that. Even with a plea of guilty to dangerous driving I had to strain to convince the trial judge that it was a case for conviction for dangerous driving. So there you are. Three cases settled at that level.

Part of the prosecutor's professional sense of independence is based on his important exercise of discretion and his supervisory control over the flow of case dispositions. Freedom to enter into negotiations with defence counsel and to accept pleas to lesser offences, to reduce charges and to withdraw charges, is a major aspect of the key position that the prosecutor plays in the administration of criminal justice. Another senior prosecutor is sensitive to this element in his work:

There is quite a lot of discretion in the prosecutor. He decides what he is going to prosecute and what cases he is going to withdraw. It's in the exercise of that discretion where difficulties can arise, because this is where the prosecution exercises a quasi-judicial and administrative function. It's one-half administrative and one-half judicial. This is where the power of the prosecution lies. It's the influences that can be brought to bear on the prosecution in that area. The prosecution must remain untrammelled in its discretion. Again, when the prosecution is in constant contact with the police, it is difficult to maintain this ideal attitude of self-determination.

The general goals and administrative values understood and accepted by those in the prosecuting unit influence their exercise of discretion. These general limitations are recognized by most prosecutors: "Again, it's a matter of getting as much as you can out of a situation. You try and get the best deal you can. You've got to please the police, and justify what you do. You don't have to check with a superior but if you are ever asked you must be able to justify what you have done."

3 THE REDUCTION OF CHARGES

Guilty pleas for consideration play a large part in the administration of criminal justice in the county of York. The reduction of a charge to a lesser offence that is included, and the reduction of the number of charges as a concession for a plea of guilty, is a major characteristic of the prosecuting process. The continual flow of guilty pleas and the corresponding avoidance of time, expense, and the uncertainty of trial are regarded by police, prosecutors, defence lawyers, and even judges as important factors in the efficient functioning of the criminal courts.

The reduction of charges to lesser offences as consideration for guilty pleas results in the disposition of a large number of cases without the usual demands on time and personnel made by the formalities of a trial. It represents an informal administrative device used to encourage guilty pleas and the consequent increased flow of case dispositions. The prosecutor will gauge his chances for success at trial on the charge originally laid against the speedy disposition of the case by a guilty plea on a reduced charge. As one prosecutor suggested: "If there is no evidence or little evidence, or when I know that the jury will most likely not convict on the charge, that is a major factor to me in taking a plea of guilty to a lesser charge. I am also interested in the likelihood of getting a conviction on the higher charge." Another said: "Or it may be just a matter of logistics and witnesses don't show up and all you can salvage is a plea to something less. It's the best you can do under the circumstances."

The number of counts or charges may be reduced for similar reasons, particularly if there has been police over-enthusiasm in charging thirty offences where ten will do. These reductions in quantity are usually painless for the prosecution since the sentence imposed by the court will not likely differ substantially because of the reduction.

If the court is going to impose the same sentence on the lesser charge as it would have on the higher charge I am just as happy with a plea of guilty to the lesser offence. If there are thirty-five counts and the accused wants to plead guilty to nine of them, I will go along if the sentence on the nine of them is going to be very similar to the sentence he would get on the thirty-five counts.

Another prosecutor indicated some factors which influence the reduction of the number of charges: "If you have thirty counts of possession, eight will do. The result is never any different and the defence can tell the client that he has made a deal. Sometimes a charge is a little thick and you'll come down."

Although the prosecution's benefits in expediting the process are considerable, the defence may not subscribe the same importance to speed. Prosecutors are aware that there must be recognizable gains for the defence from the exchange in order to perpetuate the negotiating relationship. Incentives, therefore, are offered to the defence to obtain a continuous flow of guilty pleas. "Bargaining is a tool to expedite the process and rather than just withdraw I try to get a bargain to a plea and at the same time it means that the defence can offer his client something." The reduction must be actively sought by the defence because the prosecution will rarely initiate negotiations. A prosecutor recalled:

I should have told defence counsel about the fact that I would take a plea to manslaughter without the psychiatric evidence but I never did and defence counsel never asked me if I would take a plea to manslaughter – maybe because he had little experience with murder cases. The man was convicted of non-capital murder and I was never asked about the reduction to manslaughter.

Prosecutorial promises linking reduction of sentence to an exchange for a guilty plea are minimal. Support may be given by the prosecution to the defence submissions relating to sentence, but most often the prosecutor will merely say nothing to contradict the defence plea for mitigation of the sentence. Agreements to sentence in exchange for a plea of guilty do occur, but infrequently for the judge must then be made a party to the agreement in order to assure its predictability. The attitude to agreements on sentence is summed up by one prosecutor who said: "The sentence doesn't play much part in settling them. Defence have to take their chance on sentence, but I would let them know what I was going to say as to sentence." If, in summary conviction offences and lesser traffic offences, the defence offers a plea of guilty to the lesser included offence, the reduction usually takes place. It is accepted as a policy decision made by the prosecution that when the plea to the lesser summary conviction offence is submitted it will inevitably be accepted by the prosecution. "In certain situations, it is almost automatic. For example, in impaired driving and failure to remain charges, we usually drop the failure to remain on a plea of guilty to impaired driving."

Negotiations to encourage a plea of guilty to a lesser offence may be inhibited by the public notoriety that a case has received in the press or other media. Although the prosecutor would like to accept a plea to a lesser offence the close public scrutiny awakened by the media limits his freedom of action. "If accepting a plea on a lesser offence won't shock the public conscience you may go along with it."

There are additional considerations which may influence the prosecutor's decision to exercise his discretion to reduce a charge. He may more readily agree to a compromise when he is doubtful of jury reaction because of mitigating circumstances in the case or because of the particular skill of the lawyer who will be defending the accused. Reduction may be made on compassionate grounds, in the familiar "stolen-bread-to-feed-his-family" case, or if the accused is a youthful offender, or where the charge is reduced so that the accused may be placed on probation in order that he may compensate the victim.

4 STAY OF PROCEEDINGS

In addition to the reduction of a serious offence to a lesser offence that is included, or the reduction of the number of charges outstanding against an accused, the prosecutor may exercise his discretion to "stay the proceedings." The terms "stay of proceedings" and "charge withdrawal" are not synonymous. When a charge has been withdrawn there is no charge remaining on the record, and to continue the prosecution a new charge must be laid. Consequently, the withdrawal of the charge terminates the proceedings. However, when a stay is entered the prosecutor may, at a future date, continue the proceedings without laying any new charge. Entering a stay of proceedings or *nolle prosequi* merely suspends the charge or charges. The exercise of discretion to stay proceedings is based on the power conferred by Parliament in and through the Criminal Code on the Attorney General, and delegated by him to the Crown prosecutor. It lies entirely outside the ambit of the court's authority, and when entering a stay the prosecutor does not address the court but addresses his request to the clerk of the court. The court has no part in any stay, and it is for the Attorney General to determine the course of action in regard to the future disposition of the stayed charge.[11]

11 The courts are most reluctant to interfere with the exercise of the Attorney General's discretion, even where the informant desires the continuance of the proceedings: Cf. *R.* v. *Leonard* (1962), 38 w.w.r.(n.s.) 300 (Alta.).

In a recent case[12] the Crown prosecutor directed the clerk of the court to enter a stay of proceedings after the accused had testified in his murder trial and the judge had directed the jury to return a verdict of acquittal. The trial judge received the jury's verdict of acquittal notwithstanding the stay. The British Columbia Court of Appeal ruled that once the Crown prosecutor had entered the stay, on the instructions of the Attorney General, it was beyond the trial judge's authority to accept the jury's verdict. Consequently the acquittal was a nullity. Accordingly, when the Crown immediately laid a charge of assault causing bodily harm against the accused, arising out of the same fact situation, the court ruled that the accused was not placed in double jeopardy. The court confirmed the sole discretion of the prosecutor when instructed by the Attorney General to enter a stay of proceedings. Mr Justice Bull indicated that he was not convinced of the "propriety of fairness" of the procedure taken by the Crown under these circumstances.[13]

5 WITHDRAWAL OF CHARGES

The withdrawal of a charge may take place prior to the finding of an indictment and is a complete bar to a continuation of the prosecution on that charge. A withdrawal may take place at any time after a charge has been laid. This discretionary decision made by the prosecutor is limited in practice to two general situations: withdrawals for compassionate reasons and withdrawals for police investigatory purposes. An example of a withdrawal for compassionate reasons is suggested in the following prosecutor's comment:

For example, there were a couple of kids who shinnied up a flagpole and took a couple of flags and there were also a couple of kids who took some coins from a fountain. What I do is bring them up in court with the parents and say to the magistrate, these are the facts and that is technically theft and these boys have been arrested and spent the night in jail. Usually the complainant is not interested in pursuing it and I say that the prosecution is willing to extend some leniency to the two accused and give them a chance.

12 *R.* v. *Beaudry*, [1967] 1 c.c.c. 272.
13 *Ibid.*, at p. 276. See also the recent case in the United States of *Klopher* v. *State of North Carolina* 87 s. Ct. 988 (1967) where this practice was strongly criticized.

At this stage, the magistrate usually gives the accused boys a tongue lashing and the mothers dissolve into tears and then the sheepish kids and the mothers leave the court. That's my discretion and if I have a good reason for it I go ahead and do it.

Withdrawals for compassionate reasons may be related also to certain sexual offences where, if convicted, the notoriety of the offence and the social status of the accused will likely result in suffering greatly out of proportion of the seriousness of the offence. An experienced prosecutor pointed out the circumstances under which these withdrawals take place and the implications of the exercise of his discretion to withdraw such a charge:

The main problem with defence lawyers, as far as I am concerned, or the hardest part as a prosecutor, is the exercise of your quasi-judicial function when asked to do so on no more than purely compassionate grounds. You may be asked to do it on the grounds that he is a decent young fellow and it will wreck his future and will mean he will never be able to go to the United States and, therefore, will become a second class citizen if he is convicted of an indictable offence. It becomes very hard; maybe he did it because of stupidity rather than cupidity. It's the hardest thing to say to the wife or mother or father of an accused that "I'm sorry" and that "I can't do very much." It's easier to tell a lawyer this. It makes it very hard to say I'm sorry and that I have to go through with it. Maybe I should adopt one prosecutor's attitude and that is to adhere to the book absolutely. And if a man is charged with drunk driving, it just cannot be reduced to impaired driving. I'll give you an example of these withdrawals. There was a middle-aged man who was caught in the park. The police were hiding in the bushes and they waited until the two of them were in the act and they caught them. One man was a hotel proprietor outside of town and a conviction for gross indecency – and there was no substitute charge of a lesser nature – would mean the loss of his hotel, and then he would be blacklisted as far as his liquor licence was concerned. The standard punishment, if he was convicted, for gross indecency between consenting males would be a twenty-five or fifty dollar fine and that's it. One of the accused could pay the fine and there would be no other consequences. But for this other man, he would be ruined. This was a case of two consenting males virtually in private in the bushes and they were not molesting anyone, and if I withdrew against one man I would have to withdraw against the other. When I said that I was going to withdraw these charges there was something like a palace revolution in the morality squad. The Deputy Chief of Police came over to see me and I told him that I make the decision and not the police.

Teenage misbehaviour which the arresting officer has categorized as criminal may be treated differently by the prosecutor.

When I think an accused should be treated in a lenient way, especially teenage defendants, I say something. Or I get charges withdrawn in the back room. So a kid comes and steals a few hubcaps or Coke bottles, I don't think that he should be convicted of a criminal offence. I get the parents, the police, and the lawyer (if he has one) in the back room and tell the kid that he has one strike against him and I really put the fear of God into him and then I withdraw the charge. If the police object, I try to use diplomacy. This is why I have the police there when I'm talking to the kid and I have the kid apologize to the police. The idea of justice comes in the back room. I try to frighten him. Some of the kids cry and really I guess I'm kind of holding court in my own office. I might withdraw the case quicker because of the family background. But if he has a bad background, his father isn't working and he's been hanging around on the streetcorners, I might go into the case deeper before I withdraw it. I may even remand the case for a month, to see if he behaves, and then maybe withdraw the charge after a month or two. I let the charge hang over his head ... So I try to teach him a lesson in the back room ... I don't think I'm doing wrong, at least I haven't had any complaints so far.

Prosecutors feel free to reduce or withdraw charges on their own initiative. In this way they exercise some belated control over the decision-making processes of the police. The majority of withdrawals are made on the independent initiative of the prosecutor handling the case.

There are, however, circumstances in which a prosecutor will seek the approval of the senior prosecutor before agreeing to a reduction or withdrawal. In serious charges, such as murder, or in cases which have gained public notoriety, the prosecutor will normally seek senior approval before exercising his discretion. Senior approval is also sought in most cases of police requests for the withdrawal of charges on the grounds of a proposed exchange of information by the accused. In order to minimize the purchase of immunity by known criminals, the police request is usually directed to the senior prosecutor.

Prosecutors are particularly reluctant to consent to the withdrawal of charges against informants. One prosecutor reacted strongly: "I don't like a crook buying immunity because he knows other crooks and can turn them in to save his own skin." Another reacted similarly: "The more I am pressed to withdraw, the more I push it. If the police want to protect an informer, then they shouldn't charge him." A third said: "The police attempt to withdraw charges because they say that the accused man is going to do something for the police like find some stolen goods or return some stolen bonds. But as far as I am concerned, in these cases all an accused is doing is purchasing his freedom by giving the police a payoff in a minor way." A fourth prosecutor said: "I've only been approached by the police to withdraw charges about a dozen times. Police come to you and have a girl charged with vagrancy and they ask you if you can withdraw the charge because she is going to recover something for them. These deals are usually horseshit. The officer is conned or is green enough." Another echoed the general reaction to the police requests to withdraw charges against an informer: "Hoods will steal bonds and hold them for a rainy day and then when they are charged with something they'll try to make a deal with the police to give them the bonds if the police will withdraw the charge." On the other hand a young prosecutor admitted: "I take into consideration the background of the accused and whether or not he is an informer."

The emotional attachment of the police to a particular case or their desire to protect informers for future usefulness restricts prosecutorial freedom to compromise pleas. "There may be a saw-off for an informer. You give him a little bit of a rap, but you don't put him out of circulation. So that he now knows that he can't get away with it and yet you will have his services in the future."

In charges arising out of private complaints, such as marital disputes or charges of fraud, it is the practice to address the complainant's request that the charge be withdrawn to the judge in open court. "If you are going to withdraw, you try to put it on the record why you are withdrawing the charge." This practice is followed in order to minimize the further laying of charges in private disputes. The court may wish to scrutinize with some care private complaints withdrawn because restitution has been made. The judges in the criminal courts express their reluctance to act as a "collection agency."

6 NEGOTIATION

It does not matter whether the limitations on the exercise of prosecutorial discretion to reduce or withdraw charges are imposed by policy considerations or by the co-operative attitude taken toward police requests, or even by the need for formal ratification by the court of the decision taken. They only amount to minimal restraints on the prosecutor's freedom of action in pre-trial negotiations. During that phase, crucial decisions are made which affect the future of more accused persons than those determinations made at trial. Advocacy by defence counsel at the pre-trial stage may more significantly affect the eventual outcome than his advocacy at the trial itself. Opportunities for negotiation between the defence lawyer and the prosecutor on questions of charge reduction, guilty pleas, and other available alternatives are characterized by a flexibility that does not prevail at trial. Once the trial stage is reached more rigid adversarial positions are adopted. For the informality of the pre-trial exchange between the prosecutor and defence lawyer is substituted a formality of protections, procedures, and competitive spirit that is the hallmark of the adversarial forum.

Extensive pre-trial negotiations have developed in recent years to meet the needs of the overburdened court systems in high-crime, urban centres. New administrative adjustments are made to answer new demands upon the traditional adversarial structures. For example, a jurisdiction in a large metropolitan area such as Toronto, with a high crime rate, understaffed courts, inadequate facilities, and an overburdened system, may encourage each judicial administrator from arresting officer, prosecutor, to lower court judge to expedite procedures in order to process the largest number of cases through the system with the least delay. As one young prosecutor said: "The pressure of work will cause you to accept a plea of guilty and to reduce a charge. The overloaded case load that you have is a psychological factor in making you accept a plea to a lesser offence." The prosecutor is able, in this way, to expedite the conclusion of the case with the least complication and time loss. The defence lawyer has also expedited his case with the least loss of time and money and has obtained a tangible result for his client – a reduced charge. Judicial agreement to defence-prosecution submissions is seldom refused as tangible benefits for the expedition of case backlog is a prime concern of lower court judges.

As a result of the *sub rosa* atmosphere surrounding pre-trial compromises the central concern under these circumstances is for the accuracy and fairness of the conviction procedure. There is a continuing preoccupation with the propriety of this non-judicial discretion exercised in the conviction and acquittal of defendants outside the trial process.[14] The range of inducements available to the police, the

14 See generally, D. J. Newman, *Conviction* (1966) and J. H. Skolnick, *Justice without Trial* (1966).

prosecution, and the defence counsel to encourage a plea of guilty clearly raises the spectre of an accused pleading guilty with the false hope of some goal which will remain ultimately unachieved. The inducement may also lead to the risk of an untrustworthy plea. Considerable pressure to plead guilty may be put on the accused by the accused's defence lawyer himself. Defence interest in expediting the case, particularly if unconvinced of the accused's innocence, may coincide with the interests of the prosecution.[15] The accused's own lawyer then may be the most important influence in encouraging the entry of a guilty plea.

Advice to a client to plead guilty to a lesser offence poses serious ethical problems for the defence lawyer. Assume, for example, that the charge is one of attempted murder and the prosecution's witnesses are credible but in error and that the defence must rely on a weak alibi supported by a defence witness easily impeachable on the basis of his lengthy criminal record. The prosecution may, as a result of certain doubts about the case, offer to accept a plea of guilty to assault causing bodily harm. The accused protests his innocence and is believed by his defence lawyer. At the same time if he enters a not guilty plea to attempted murder his lawyer honestly predicts his conviction and sentence of ten or fifteen years. Whereas, if a plea of guilty is entered to assault causing bodily harm no more than a one-year sentence is predicted and there is some likelihood of a suspended sentence. If the defence lawyer is convinced of his client's innocence, should he convey the prosecution's offer to him and suggest its acceptance?[16]

The inducements and reductions available in one prosecutorial jurisdiction may not resemble those available in another. An urban jurisdiction with the burden of a heavy case load may engage in expediting procedures unheard of in a neighbouring prosecutorial office that is not subject to the same administrative strains. Differing policies of pre-trial negotiation may depend on the demands of the locality. The severely punitive habitual criminal legislation may be threatened and enforced in one jurisdiction, whereas the policy in another jurisdiction may be to ignore these provisions. This lack of a consistent pattern of

15 See Blumberg, "The Practice of Law as a Confidence Game: Organizational Co-optation of a Profession," 1 L. & Soc. Rev. 15 (1967).
16 See Freedman, "Professional Responsibility of the Criminal Defence Lawyer: The Three Hardest Questions," 64 Mich. L. Rev. 1469, at p. 1480–1 (1966).

prosecutorial enforcement policies leads to an image of capriciousness incompatible with public or official expectations of certainty in the criminal law. Abuses of discretion for political reasons were not evident in the office studied. But no matter how high the level of the quality of the prosecuting personnel, such suspicions cannot be avoided when the exercise of discretion is the individual prerogative of each prosecutor.

The adversarial forum provides procedural protections and an open atmosphere where evidentiary rules and judicial control insure the fairness of the proceedings. In the pre-trial process these same protections are unavailable. Moreover, in Canada the indigent accused is often unrepresented by a defence lawyer prior to his trial.[17] The unequal bargaining position between an unrepresented accused unfamiliar with pre-trial opportunities and the police and prosecution is obvious. Opportunity to utilize the variety of pre-trial alternatives is available to those who are represented by counsel and unavailable to others who are not. Since the prosecutor will rarely initiate negotiations himself, familiarity with the negotiating practices of the jurisdiction and skilled advocacy is required in order to benefit from pre-trial concessions.

Association of accused persons with the pre-trial negotiating environment imprints upon them a conception of criminal prosecution as a system which is subject to manipulation by those experienced at the game to the exclusion of those who are not. This perspective engenders little respect for the administration of criminal law and creates correctional and rehabilitory problems. Donald Newman stressed the importance of the way in which accused persons perceive their treatment within the criminal law processes when he wrote: "Correctional personel feel that it is desirable for an offender to enter the correctional process convinced that he has had his day in court, that all officials have acted fairly and decently to him, that his side of the story has been heard, and that he has not been railroaded or cheated of his rights in any way."[18]

17 For a discussion of the right to counsel in Canada, see Grosman, "The Right to Counsel in Canada," 10 *Can. Bar J.* 189 (1967).
18 Newman, *Conviction*, at p. 44.

CHAPTER FIVE

The Administrative
Perspective

1 THE POLICE: INFLUENCE AND PRESSURE

Police decisions to arrest and charge not only define the outer limits of law enforcement policy, but, as we have noted, control the initial decision to prosecute. Failure by prosecuting authorities to provide machinery to screen charges by making available appropriate legal advice at the early charging stages is one cause of the pervasive police influence over the initiation of prosecutions. Police decisions to charge, however, represent only part of the general influence that the police exercise over the prosecution of criminal offences.

The high degree of occupational solidarity among the police strengthens their conception of their role as professionals charged alone with the enforcement of the law.[1] The decision to arrest is, in most situations, made only when the police officer has decided that the accused is guilty of the offence for which he is being arrested. Since the arresting officer has made his assessment of the accused's guilt at the time he has made the arrest, he will often perceive subsequent procedural requirements and the protections accorded the accused in the legal environment as frustrating the orderly and efficient administration of justice. If he, as a professional law enforcement agent, had not believed the accused guilty he would not have arrested him. Jerome Skolnick has pointed

---

1 W. A. Westley, "The Police: A Sociological Study of Law, Custom and Morality," 1951 (unpublished PH D thesis, University of Chicago). Westley has examined the influences of the policeman's occupational environment upon his work habits.

out the nature of the police officers' presumption in his study of the police:

In contrast to the criminal law presumption that a man is innocent until proven guilty the policeman tends to maintain an administrative presumption of regularity, in effect, a presumption of guilt. When he makes an arrest and decides to book a suspect, the officer feels that the suspect has committed the crime charged. He believes that as a specialist in crime, he has the ability to distinguish between guilt and innocence.[2]

The police have difficulty distinguishing between factual and legal guilt. Once they have made the assessment of the accused's factual guilt the legal protections, evidentiary requirements, and the presumptions favouring the accused at trial are seen primarily as obstacles to efficient law enforcement. Professor Skolnick distinguishes evaluative standards of the police from those of the courts: "Because he is enmeshed in a network of professional responsibilities and values not shared by judges, the policeman fails to respond to judicial interpretations of legality. Instead his allegiance is to the police organization and its evaluative standards."[3]

Police bias is acknowledged by most prosecutors and it is explicable by the occupational perspectives of the police which ascribe the highest priority to "crime fighting" and the arrest of the guilty. Emotional attachment to a case and police pursuit of conviction is particularly manifest where it is alleged that a sexual offence has been committed against a young child or where the police have been physically or verbally abused by the accused during arrest. In addition, when police have invested substantial investigatory effort and have arrested a notorious or important suspect, they are much more interested in the successful prosecution and conviction of the accused than they are in the case of more routine arrests.[4] On the other hand, when an informer has been charged, often as a result of poor interdepartmental communication, the police, in the interests of continued efficient enforcement, demonstrate an unwillingness to allow a useful informer to be placed behind bars. How do police values, their emotional attachment to cases, and

2 Skolnick, *Justice without Trial* (1966), at p. 187.
3 *Ibid.*, at p. 227.
4 Westley, "The Police," at pp. 10–11, 201–10, and 223–4.

their administrative bias influence prosecutorial behaviour? What pressures do they place on the prosecution by their presumption that "we do not arrest innocent people"?

The police and the prosecution must engage in day-to-day contact because of the policeman's position as the prosecution's chief informant and prime witness. The administrative demands and the pressure of the case load force the prosecutor to rely heavily and often exclusively on police advice and information since independent sources of information about the accused, the facts of the case, and the charges are unavailable at this stage. "The police prepare the dope sheet," said one prosecutor, "and we are dependent on it to prepare our case. We don't examine the information in the cases because in order to examine the information that is filed in court we would need half as many prosecutors again ..." As a result, police information and fact appraisal dominate the prosecuting process in the lower courts.

As a consequence of the prosecutor's reliance on the police, a relationship of trust often develops between them. The operational biases of the police become contagious in a necessarily intimate relationship. A prosecutor indicated some of the inherent problems:

The police and the prosecution are thrown together. Ideally, the prosecution should be a buffer between the police and the public but necessarily the prosecution has to rely on the police. There is a danger because the prosecutor comes to accept blindly what he is told. Personal friendships develop with the officers since you see them every day and you tend to accept what they tell you. You've got a duty to the police and the public to see that people who break the law get prosecuted and if the evidence is there, that they be convicted. At the same time, you have a duty to the public at large. When you are thrown into constant contact with the police it's difficult to do both duties. It's something you have to guard against. You have to try to err on the side of the public rather than the police. This is a danger that the system lends itself to.

Most prosecutors carefully distinguished the interests of the police from those of the prosecution: "We are not counsel for the police; we are naturally pleading the cause in which the police are interested; we are not on the police side as a policeman."

Informational resources are limited at the lower-court level. Police information is accepted without adequate confirmation. "There is a large measure of trust between the prosecutor and the police. You have to take what they tell you on trust." Most prosecutors acknowledged police advocacy but did not acknowledge that the police point of view significantly influenced their own perspective. "The police often try to influence you, and it is entirely understandable. They tend to feel strongly about their cases and know in their own mind that the accused is guilty and try to instill their beliefs in the prosecution." Others recognized the influence of police persuasiveness:

I like to think that they are just complainants but because of the frequency of working with them – try to remember that I'm not a lawyer for the police – it's very easy to find yourself prosecuting for the police rather than the state. Some police are very persuasive and you might work harder on their case than if you had a police officer who wasn't so persuasive.

2 REACTION TO POLICE PRESSURE

It is in the lower courts that police advocacy and their professional commitment is most apparent. Since those prosecuting in the magistrates' courts are often inexperienced and have little time available for preparation, they rely on senior police officers for guidance as well as information. Neophyte prosecutors are most susceptible to police pressure and easily influenced by the occupational perspective of the police.

When you first join the prosecution staff, the police make an effort to ask you to go out with them on a night run, particularly the morality squad which might raid a bawdy house; it's sort of becoming part of the investigation. "If you could have seen the victim," the police often say ... because they feel quite often you become more sympathetic to their point of view if you see the results of the offence involved. Then you will be on their side ...

A prosecutor with substantial experience pointed out the problems a young prosecutor faces in his relations with the police:

When a proseuctor is young he has certain problems with the police. Typical of these problems is a police officer who comes in to a young prosecutor and says, "we haven't any evidence and we want the charge withdrawn." Then the prosecutor withdraws because he is overawed by the police or by the rank of the individual police officer. An older prosecutor would not go for that. With a young fellow the police ask for exhorbitant bail for no reason except that charges are outstanding or use the excuse they are about to lay other charges or that they are continuing the investigation or something like that. A young fellow might go along with the police and support their request for a very high bail. When a young prosecutor comes into the office he is inclined, when he first comes here, to be impressed with a facet of life he knows nothing about. For example, in the book-making aspect of things, the police may give the prosecutor the feeling that this is highly organized and dangerous and the police might make you a crusader in order to make you participate in the prevention or the detection of crime. They mould a lot of your thinking. You forget you are an advocate or a barrister and you start fighting the cause of the police. Young prosecutors tend to drink with the police and to fraternize with them and think the police are really good fellows and they adopt the police point of view. This changes when you realize that their judgment is faulty. ... The prosecutor is to be a buffer between the police and the public – the police take themselves a bit too seriously and have little sense of proportion and excessive zeal and dedication or lack of discretion and lay charges where there is no purpose in charges being laid.

Another senior prosecutor reacted to police pressure in the following way:

Also with the police you have to show them who's boss. Once they understand that, they might not like your call on a thing ... I'll give them the reasons ... if they don't like it, it's too damn bad. They suggest bail on the sheets. They pick it out of a hat, $2,000, $3,000, $4,000; I call it the way I see it. I had a few blowups but I left no doubt as to who was calling the shot. I'm the guy who has to take the responsibility for the call so I make the decision.

Acceptance of police attitudes and commitments were particularly noticeable among those prosecutors who had moved from their law school education directly into the prosecutor's office. Their professional perspectives were moulded by their early formative contact with senior police officers and fellow prosecutors.[5] A young prosecutor, appointed directly from law school, spoke of his relations with the police:

There are no problems. I am generally inclined to believe the police. I believe that most people in the criminal courts know why they are there and their only regret is that they are caught. The police approach which says that they know what they are doing is, in my opinion, a realistic approach. In most cases I agree with the police. There are no means of independent investigation by our office and we have to rely on the police and it depends how much trust you put into the police force, and I put a great deal of trust into the police force. I guess sometimes there are abuses and the prosecution doesn't see the whole picture, but for the most part I trust the police.

His acceptance of the professional commitment and perspective of the police seriously limits the efficacy of his independent status within the legal, as distinct from the police, environment. Unless his goals have been clearly formulated by past associations and education prior or external to his prosecuting engagements, his position will gain its meaning from this occupational environment.

In the higher courts police pressures are minimal. The diminution of police pressure at the higher judicial level may result in part from the resistance encountered by the police from the more experienced prosecutors who conduct trials at this level, and in part from the independent judgment exercised by the same prosecutors based, as it is, on the availability of adequate time and sources of information for the preparation of the case. It was suggested by a prosecutor who is engaged primarily in trials in the higher courts that the relationship with the police prevalent in the lower courts withers in the atmosphere of the higher court: "When you move out of magistrates' court and up to the assizes, you get out of the police element and you begin to realize that you are a lawyer and the relationship changes. Only when you get away from the police influence which pervades the magistrates' courts does the relationship change.

3 MANAGEMENT

Daily administrative contacts with police and defence lawyers outside the adversarial arena absorb the greater part of the prosecutor's working day. His administrative routine and work significantly affect his professional commitment. It is important, then, to consider his daily duties and their influence on his professional perspective.

If the prosecutor is assigned to a magistrates' court he begins each morning before entering the courtroom by inspecting the day's court list with a senior police officer responsible for police-prosecutor liaison. The liaison officer will, in the short space of time available prior to the opening of court, attempt to brief the prosecutor on a number of matters of importance for the morning's proceedings. For example, they will quickly consider those cases that will be adjourned at the request of the defence to another day, those cases which will proceed, those where a defence lawyer will be present to represent the accused, those where a plea of guilty will likely be entered, and those which must be adjourned because the police or Crown witnesses are unavailable. The liaison officer will summarily explain the major characteristics of the cases which will likely proceed and, with the prosecutor, will inspect the "dopesheet" which sets out a synopsis of the facts prepared by the police.

Once the prosecutor enters the magistrates' courtroom, those defence lawyers who wish to arrange remands, bail, pleas to lesser offences, and who would ascertain the prosecutor's intentions with regard to their client, will engage him in a brief dialogue. Discussions of this nature often take place in the brief interval between the prosecutor's arrival in the courtroom and the magistrate's entry a few moments later. The remainder of the morning is spent in court speaking first to the adjournments, then to the guilty pleas, and finally prosecuting the one or two cases which may proceed to trial before the magistrate. In the afternoon the prosecution may contact Crown witnesses for trials which will proceed the following day or conduct a preliminary hearing. Those who are prosecuting cases in the higher courts spend a greater proportion of their time arranging for witnesses and carefully constructing the calendar of cases.

The prosecutor assigned to a particular courtroom must arrange the order of the cases to be heard at the sitting of the court. In addition he must arrange for backup cases. If a case is "settled" by the entry of a plea of guilty just prior to or at trial another case must be readied immediately to proceed. The backup case must be one of some simplicity, not requiring extensive preparation. It must depend, for the most part, on police evidence as other witnesses will be unavailable on short notice. The prosecutor constructs the calendar of cases to be heard in the courtroom two weeks prior to the commencement of the term. He knows then the nature of the cases coming before the judge and he is aware also of the number of cases he must deal with during the sitting. Careful planning and administration is required in order to avoid the possibility of a judge sitting ready to try a case when there is no case readily available for trial. The existence of a sizeable case backlog in Toronto demands that the judge have a continual stream of cases before him without any substantial delay between the disposition of one case and the initiation of the hearing in another.

4 THE TIME MACHINE

In all the criminal courts the prosecutor's major administrative responsibility is to ensure that the cases before the court keep moving. Keen determination to ensure the smooth functioning of the process characterizes much of the prosecutor's work. He has been likened to the guardian of a funnel, whose major task it is to make certain the funnel is not blocked.[6] Cases must proceed efficiently to determination. The prime administrative value is celerity, the need to dispose of a great number of cases with the least delay. Delay not only means that cases may have to be put over to the following assize, a delay of one or two months, but also results in the discontent of judges who must deal with a growing case backlog. Delays force upon the prosecutor the unpleasant task of offering explanations to defence lawyers, judges, and witnesses who are waiting to proceed.

A particularly difficult administrative problem resulting from delay concerns the availability and enthusiasm of prosecution witnesses. Not only are Crown witnesses reluctant to return to the courthouse day after day without testifying but their enthusiasm diminishes considerably after they have been called from their employment and then find that the case has been delayed or adjourned and that they must, at some later date, again leave their employment to testify. Prosecution witnesses may have commitments that take them out of the city or on holidays, thus interfering with their extended availability. Under these circumstances Crown evidence cools quickly.

Delay generally works for the defence and seriously impedes the prosecution. This accounts for the particular frustration felt by prosecutors, for delay not only impedes the smooth administrative disposition of the greatest number of cases in the shortest possible time, but

6 See Skolnick, "Social Control in the Adversary System," 11 *J. Conflict Resolution* 52, at p. 56 (1967).

it directly affects the continued viability of the prosecution's evidence against the accused. One prosecutor, describing the problems said:

A prosecutor is orientated on a volume basis, and the volume of work that you have and can do is a prime consideration. You try and pick out the meat of a case and reduce it, and it irritates a prosecutor that defence counsel don't adopt the same attitude. By and large, defence are not moved by the same considerations and are inclined to waste a lot of time, raising alternative defences, etc. This makes for disagreement because of the time element.

Another prosecutor voiced his frustration: "It's a pain in the neck having defence counsel running over all the evidence in all the cases. We have five hundred or six hundred cases a day in this building and one or two long-winded defence counsel plug up the list. I suppose it's a cross we have to bear."

To encourage the disposition of the greatest number of cases with the least complication and delay the prosecutor relies on the informality and flexibility of pre-trial negotiations and resorts to the compromise of cases in exchange for guilty pleas. On the one hand, the guilty plea represents the most expedient manner by which to dispose of the greatest number of cases with the least administrative complication and delay; the formal trial, on the other, consumes an unpredictable length of time with the concomitant inconvenience to prosecution witnesses, police officers, as well as to counsel and accused persons who are awaiting the trial of their cases. The preoccupation with maintaining celerity and avoiding delay colours the prosecutor's perspective and gives rise to a number of practical adjustments to meet pressing administrative needs.

The pace of criminal prosecution encourages a number of time-saving administrative expedients. A lower court judge, when asked to make a decision on the question of bail, usually accepts the suggestion of the prosecutor. The decision whether bail should be granted and the determination of the amount required is, in law, the sole function of the judge.[7] Unfortunately, the judge has little time available at this

7 C.C. S.S. 463, 464, and see *Re Sommervill's Prohibition Application* (1962), 38 W.W.R.(n.s.) 344, at p. 352: "The agents and officers of the Department of the Attorney-General have the right on any such application to make such representations as they see fit to the presiding magistrate in court, but they do not have 'a scintilla of right' to hinder or delay the making of the application or to instruct a magistrate as to what his decision should be in any judicial matter."

stage to conduct an inquiry by assessing independent sources of information. As a result prosecutors can confidently assert: "The judges usually do whatever you say in regard to bail." The prosecutor's recommendation itself is not the product of independent information relating to the roots of the accused in the community. Because of the need for a speedy decision it is often based on the advice of the police officer in charge of the case, or the court liaison officer.[8] "On bail, the police have the most influence because they advise you about a guy's past."

The one criteria recognized in law for determining the requirement and amount of bail is the likelihood that the accused, if released on bail, will appear voluntarily in court at the time of his trial.[9] In practice, the factors which influence the prosecutor's recommendation in regard to bail are the following, in descending order of importance: the police recommendation, the criminal record of the accused, the seriousness of the offence, the likelihood of the commission of further offences if the accused is released on bail, the likelihood of the accused tampering with witnesses if released on bail, the roots of the accused in the community, and his physical appearance. In many ways the time available dictates the limitations under which a prosecutor must learn to work. Because of the lack of independent sources of information available for bail applications and the need to make an immediate decision, the prosecutor utilizes criteria and information which are immediately available to him. Even the physical appearance of the accused becomes relevant under these circumstances: "I take into consideration his appearance, whether he is well dressed and looks like he is established in the community – if he is dressed like a bum it is likely he is a bum."

The continual and pressing nature of the prosecutor's administrative duties and the number of cases on the court list encourages an administrative perspective based primarily on expediting values – the need to deal with the given case load in the shortest time possible. This perspective weakens the competitive adversarial positions and adds to the

8 See generally, for an excellent account of bail practices in Canada, M. Friedland, *Detention Before Trial* (1965).
9 For a statement of the principles in the granting of bail, see *R.* v. *Wing*, [1964] 3 c.c.c. 102, disapproving *R.* v. *Henderson* (1963), 45 w.w.r.(n.s.) 55. And see also *Rodway and Okipnik* v. *R.* (1964), 44 c.r. 327 and *R.* v. *Johnson's Bail Application* (1958), 26 w.w.r.(n.s.) 296, 29 c.r. 138, 122 c.c.c. 144.

attractions of conciliatory practices which circumvent the obstacles and delays inherent in a resort to the adversarial contest. As a result of the pressures inherent in his work the prosecutor is not primarily interested in winning cases at trial. He is most interested in disposing of cases efficiently. This is particularly evident in his lack of interest in the sentencing process. Once the case has been determined, the prosecution usually displays little interest in the sentence imposed by the court, unless the case has gained some notoriety or it is felt that the sentence is clearly not "in line" with the seriousness of the offence. This rarely occurs. The prosecutor's reluctance to speak to sentence unless requested to do so by the judge seems general.

Only if the defence made inaccurate submissions would I contradict those submissions. Most of the time I say nothing as to sentence and only if I am asked for a submission will I give it.

It is my habit on sentence to read the accused's record and to sit down and I seldom say anything as to sentence.

I feel that it is wrong for the prosecution to speak to sentence. We are not qualified to assist the court in imposing sentence. What right have I got to suggest the quantum. What right have I got? I'm no penologist. I don't know this man. It's no part of my business. It's not a job for a lawyer.

The number of cases lost at trial do not cause as much concern to prosecutors as the number of cases which ultimately proceed to trial.

A manager or supervisor charged with responsibility for the efficient processing of goods from reception to finished product is unlikely, if the backlog on the assembly line threatens to jam up the production system, to concern himself with high but imprecise standards of quality control imposed by some external body remote from the exigencies of the plant procedures. He will process the goods quickly, responding to the pressing production demands. Once these have been met and production proceeds at a more leisurely pace, he may consider more carefully the quality of the product and whether it is meeting certain standards, in order to live up to the ideals of the industry. Unfortunately, production seldom slows down, and the manager has little time for the luxury of contemplating the sometimes unrealistic goals of the industry.

Similarly, the prosecutor who acts as a supervisor of the progress of criminal cases from inception to disposition reacts to the demands of the system as any competent manager might. Since the demands of the prosecutor's managerial role include substantial administrative and supervisory duties, it is not surprising that his attitudes reflect the nature of his work. Accordingly, there is little time available for concern over standards of due process or for the protections available to an accused. If due process standards or protections seriously impede the system's capacity to determine efficiently the large number of cases continually flowing into it, the protections will often fall victim to the administrative demands and the pressures of production.

Sometimes there is evidence available that is not on the dope sheet or is not reaching my ears. There are some things I would just as soon not know about. A certain percentage of the statements are obtained improperly and if it comes to my attention I won't allow them in, but I don't cross examine the police officer on whether a statement is improper or not before I introduce it. But we know that there are statements that are taken improperly and certain police officers perjure themselves.

5 THE ADMINISTRATIVE PERSPECTIVE VS PROCEDURAL PROTECTIONS

A similar reluctance by prosecutors to implement due process standards was displayed in their answers to the question whether they believed an accused man should have a right to representation by counsel before trial:

What does he need a lawyer for, before trial? All a lawyer is going to tell him is to shut up and fall on the floor.

I believe there is a psychological compulsion on an accused to get it off his chest, and having a lawyer at this first instance would not be beneficial to police investigation.

I heard the Deputy Chief say that to have a lawyer before trial is obstructing justice and some of the prosecutors feel the same way.

As soon as these guys are arrested they want to phone a lawyer and that impedes investigation. If you let that happen you would have chaos.

These and similar reactions were characteristic of most young prosecutors who had arrived directly from law school, and a few of the older men who had not engaged in the practice of law outside the prosecutors' office. It is these same prosecutors who suggested that it is not their function to inquire behind the evidence gathered by the police, and that they are merely to prosecute those cases that come before them and not to initiate an inquiry into the method by which the evidence was obtained. It was the young career prosecutors who identified most strongly with the police administrative perspective and who adopted as their prime value the protection of the community and the need to fight crime. As a "crime-fighter" they are opposed to what are considered the "inordinate protections" available to the accused:

If an accused has a lawyer as soon as he is being investigated by the police, the lawyer will try to prevent the conviction of his client and his obvious advice is shut up and say nothing. The protection of the community is opposed to that. My opinion is that the presence of defence counsel at that stage of the proceedings is detrimental to the process.

Well, I don't agree with advising an accused of his right to counsel at a station house. It is difficult enough to combat crime and this would mean that there would be fewer statements.

However, those prosecutors who had gained some practical experience prior to joining the office of the prosecutor seemed to take a somewhat different approach to the question of whether the accused should be entitled the advice of counsel prior to trial:

I agree with it absolutely. Why shouldn't they? If they make a request for a lawyer, they should be given an opportunity to get the lawyer at the point when they make that request.

If a man asks for a lawyer he has a right to see him. Yes, any time.

If he asks for a lawyer, sure, why not? That's the rules of the game. If they haven't got enough evidence without depending on the statement, if they need the statement in order to get a conviction, it's a weak case and they should go out and get the evidence.

If an accused does request counsel, normally a concerted effort will be made by the judge or the local legal aid association to see that he is represented at trial. On the other hand, if the accused either through ignorance or bravado does not request the assistance of counsel, none will be provided for him. One prosecutor suggested that the absence of counsel prior to trial or at trial was of no assistance to successful prosecution:

There is no doubt that there is a right to counsel at the trial. The accused should be allowed to get in touch with his counsel. It would save us a lot of grief if counsel was present. We've had counsel present during a line-up or an impaired driving test and if he sees that everything is in order he can't later object to it. If the officer at the station won't let the accused call a lawyer it taints the whole prosecution. There is nothing worse than trying to prosecute a person who doesn't have counsel either at the preliminary hearing or at the trial. And it is impossible before a jury.

Once again the prosecutor's primary concern is with the delay and administrative confusion that arises from the lack of representation. The rights of the accused, and the unfairness of procedures where his protections remain dormant in the absence of competent counsel, seem of little importance. The moral question is never raised. Should a man, who at this stage is presumed innocent, be refused the protections that only representation by defence counsel can provide? There is general agreement that an accused should be represented by counsel at the trial, otherwise the trial will be inordinately delayed by the accused's unfamiliarity with procedures and by the need to engage in continual explanations and interpretations on his behalf. At the same time representation by counsel prior to trial is viewed as a serious impediment to police investigation and efficient prosecution.

The same remoteness from the accused and his protections is reflected in the prosecutors' attitudes towards the pre-trial imprisonment of those persons who are unable to raise the required bail. Detention of an accused in the local jail prior to trial is said by some prosecutors to serve a number of useful purposes in addition to assuring his attendance at trial. "In some cases, it tends to wear them down. After the fourth remand, they are likely to cop out in some cases." Pre-trial imprisonment may encourage an accused to plead guilty or, even if not convicted, may serve as a useful lesson. "In the case of a young fellow I feel a couple of days in jail, for a student, might help him to smarten up. It also serves the purpose that if the police want to question him, he's available."

In law, prior to a finding of guilt by legally constituted authority, there is a continuing presumption of the accused's innocence. This presumption adheres to the accused until blameworthiness is assessed by the only authority competent to do so, the judiciary. And yet, the majority of the prosecutors assumed the factual reliability of the police decision to initiate the prosecution. When characterizing the accused prior to the court's assessment of guilt or innocence in law, the prosecutor assumes the accused's guilt in fact: "The presumption of innocence as far as I am concerned is an evidentiary device and I would have to be mad to think that some of these people were innocent until the time they were convicted." This prosecutorial position is consistent with the presumption of administrative regularity: "We don't arrest innocent people."

In order to "fight crime" the criminal administrative process must function smoothly and those arrested must be expediently convicted within the context of a mass system for the administration of criminal law. The law is perceived, not primarily as an instrument for guaranteeing individual freedom, but as a means of protecting public order and preserving the efficient administration of justice.[10] Those who have been arrested are presumed guilty and it is the prosecutor's duty to process them. He processes bodies rather than individuals. Considerable remoteness from the accused and his plight is current and, indeed, is encouraged as a healthy professional adjustment: "The accused man? You couldn't care less after a while. It's pretty hard to work up much enthusiasm after your twentieth indecent assault in a row. You get dull and stale and he (the accused) is just another face in the crowd. He is number 656 on the list ..." In a process so closely concerned with people, human and individualistic elements of those persons in trouble with the law are minimized, and persons become objects and products which must be processed through the system. The prosecuting system acts as an effective machine for the production of convictions and the processing and disposition of convicted persons into institutions set up to deal with them. The chief aim of the system is to control the efficiency of the process and guarantee the continuance of the stream without inordinate delay and complication. The accused becomes humanized only when he causes delays and difficulties and inhibits the smooth

10 See Packer, "Two Models of the Criminal Process," 113 U. of Pa. L. Rev. 1 (1964) for an excellent analysis of what he describes as the "crime control model" and the "due process model."

functioning of the process. Otherwise, he remains a number: "You never see the accused during the trial because he is behind you. He becomes just a name on the file. It's like dropping bombs from fifty thousand feet up – you have little contact with the humans below."

The police and the prosecutors interpret procedural requirements as frustrating the efficient administration of criminal justice. This interpretation is reflected in most of the responses of prosecutors and their consistent assumption of the need for administrative regularity. Procedural protections, such as the presence of counsel prior to arraignment, are seen as contributing to the frustration of those charged with the investigation and prosecution of crime. The prosecutor's easy acceptance of an accused's imprisonment prior to trial is understandable if one views that acceptance in the light of his presumption of administrative regularity and his corresponding presumption of the accused's probable guilt. As soon as the accused enters the prosecuting system by arrest, the administrative perspective of police and prosecutors begins to operate. His arrest is *prima facie* evidence that he is guilty and that he must be the kind of person who should be in the system. He is identified as an offender and the chief aim of the prosecution is to control his progress through the stages of prosecution in a manageable way. Depersonalization and professional remoteness avoid any moralistic interpretations of the accused's behaviour and ambivalent attitudes on the part of the prosecutor which would complicate his functional role.

CHAPTER SIX

The Professional
Perspective

1 WHO ARE PROSECUTORS?

The Crown Attorney's office in the county of York was growing rapidly at the time this study was made and four additional assistant prosecutors were added in a six-month period. These new appointees arrived directly from law school with no interval of professional experience in private practice prior to their appointment. This was characteristic of most of the recent appointments. In contrast, the prosecutors appointed four or five years prior to the study were mostly men who had gained some experience in private practice before their appointment. They had come, for the most part, from Anglo-Saxon, Protestant, upper class families with a private school education; thus, they were men from homogeneous milieus which did not resemble the variety of religious and ethnic affiliations characteristic of the most recent additions.

Whether the new appointee arrived directly from law school or had spent a number of years in professional practice, in most cases his academic record was not distinguished. At that time, the prosecutor's office was attracting neither the best law students nor the most successful practitioners into the field of criminal prosecutions. This may have been partly because for many years the salary range was lower than the remuneration that a lawyer of equivalent years could expect to earn in private practice. Too often it meant that accepting a position as an assistant Crown Attorney resulted in a substantial financial sacrifice. Consequently, applications may have been limited to those of independent means or those who had little hope of successful earnings in private practice and accordingly sought the security offered by the position. Today, salary scales have been improved and earnings are not substantially out of line with salaries paid to lawyers of similar experience in large legal firms in the city.[1]

Young law graduates who wish eventually to engage in criminal trial practice are attracted to the office of the prosecutor for it provides them with intensive experience in the criminal courts and with an opportunity to meet those engaged in the defence-prosecuting community. Many of the young appointees view the office not as the goal of a permanent career but as a temporary training ground, and as an introduction to a criminal practice which assures the benefits of organizational and financial security. They are primarily interested in gaining criminal court experience. The low level of career motivation is indicated by the remarks of one young prosecutor: "I cast around for a job ... and decided that the prosecutor's office was a good place to start, that it would provide good experience." Another said: "So I decided to try law for a year or so and kept trying. I was never a very good student. The last thing in the world I intended to be was a Crown prosecutor."

Very few who were attracted to the office said they were highly motivated although there were one or two exceptions: "I have always been interested in trial work, especially criminal trials, and I used to come down to the courthouse to watch cases when I was in high school. It was my hobby even before I got to university; I used to sit in court and I was always interested in the prosecution of criminal cases." Once engaged in prosecution some said they found considerable satisfactions although there was little consensus about their nature. The same prosecutor who said "it was my hobby" suggested that his enthusiasm has never waned: "After seven years I'm still enjoying it. There is lots of

1 See schedule of fees for Crown Attorneys in Ontario, in 2 Ontario Royal Commission Inquiry into Civil Rights, *Report no. 1*, 940 (1968). For a historical survey of the emoluments of the law officers of the Crown in England see J. Ll. J. Edwards, *Law Officers of the Crown*, 69–118 (1964). Compare salaries in the United States collected by D. R. Nedrud, "The Career Prosecutor," 1959 (unpublished thesis, Northwestern University School of Law), where it is pointed out that in some states permanent prosecutors augment their inadequate salaries by a percentage of the fines collected or by fees paid only when a conviction is obtained.

variety and you deal with people and there is lots of court work." Another suggested: "I am completely happy because I like the action. Every day is different. It is not a routine existence."

Professional legal education is deemed sufficient training to qualify for appointment to the position of prosecutor. It is believed that specialized skills in prosecuting will be acquired on the job where colleagues and senior police officers play a major role in interpreting the prosecutor's role to the novice. The young prosecutor begins his on-the-job training at the lowest prestige level, the "impaired driving" court, and will, after a few months, conduct cases in the general magistrates' courts where he may also conduct preliminary inquiries. After a year or two he will be moved up to conduct trials in the general sessions and eventually appear before the Supreme Court at the assizes. This hierarchical transition represents a succession of rewards for professional skills displayed at the lower levels. The conduct of prosecutions in the higher courts is considered more prestigious than prosecution at the magistrates' court level: "Guys at the bottom don't do the interesting stuff."

2 WHAT IT TAKES TO SUCCEED

While the office of the prosecutor is considered an excellent training ground for a young lawyer, the lack of adequate time for preparation at the lower levels encourages a certain rough and ready approach to representation in the lower courts: "It's no place for somebody who needs hours to prepare things. You have to make snap decisions and usually on your feet ..." The continual stream of cases, particularly in the magistrates' courts, creates a somewhat frenetic atmosphere not conducive to a contemplative consideration of the individual merits of each case.

He should be thick-skinned, this is pretty important. If not, the pressure of work and the split second decisions you have to make on your feet in magistrates' court would really bother you. The defence football huddle around the prosecutor when he comes in at ten o'clock in the morning and the yak of the police and magistrates and the hurly burly of the magistrates' court; if you were sensitive you would have an ulcer. You have to learn to make up your mind quickly and you need a form of aggressiveness.

Another prosecutor suggested that the kind of man best equipped for the job "would need to be able to withstand pressure, the pressure of having to prosecute cases where you are not familiar or prepared. He would have to be prepared to ... lose cases. If he is a man who has to succeed every time, he had better stay away from it."

In the courtroom there is the acknowledged pressure that, once adversarial positions have been taken and a trial takes place, "You can't afford to have too many people found not guilty. Better not to prosecute them in the first place." The pressure to succeed at trial is twofold. To maintain his administrative credibility and to encourage guilty pleas the prosecutor must demonstrate that he is able if forced to take the final adversarial remedy, to succeed consistently at trial. If he were continually defeated the compromises offered in pre-trial negotiations would quickly lose their value. The defence would be risking little by advising the entry of a not guilty plea if a complete acquittal at trial seemed probable. Too many prosecutions lost at trial seriously undermine faith in the competency and decision-making of the initiators. Successes, as well as confirming administrative regularity, are needed to justify the confidence placed by most prosecutors in the professional soundness of the original initiating decision by the police, and to corroborate their conviction that most persons accused of crime are guilty. One prosecutor, when asked whether there was any pressure to produce, replied:

You mean successes? Yes, I think there is. It stems from the realization of those in office for some time that people before the courts are justly accused of their wrongdoing. By coincidence, once in a while you get a string of not guilty cases but if it persists for too long maybe you are not prosecuting with vigour. The reason for it is a general feeling that before someone is charged there is evidence indicative that they committed the offence with which they are charged. There is a feeling that if you have been going for quite a while with few convictions there is something wrong.

The viability of the administrative perspective that "we don't arrest innocent people" can only be sustained if the vast majority of cases are either disposed of by guilty pleas or convictions at trial. As another prosecutor said: "Ninety-five per cent of the people are guilty as charged. Those cases that are thrown out are thrown out mostly on evidentiary gaps in the Crown's case." In sum, confidence in present administrative practices is maintained only if the acquittal rate is not substantial. In that sense prosecutors see themselves as engaged competing not directly with defence lawyers but to sustain their own record and credibility.

3 THE ATTRACTIONS OF PROSECUTION

The rewards of status, the attractions and satisfactions connected with the office of the prosecutor, are not uniformly perceived by all or most prosecutors; instead, their relative importance depends on subjective evaluations of individual members. They reach their judgments in the light of, and with reference to, the attractions and benefits they believe to be attainable by fellow lawyers in other areas of professional practice. Any report of the motivations and emotional satisfactions felt by the prosecutors in the county of York must necessarily employ psychological, indeed psycho-analytic, techniques. Such probings are beyond the scope of this inquiry. As a result it is only the prosecutors' verbal rationalizations and manifestations of their observable behaviour which must serve, for our purposes, as an outline of those attractions and satisfactions of the office which are openly acknowledged.

The attractions of the prosecutorial office and its satisfactions are seldom restricted to the evident training opportunities, the relative freedom from supervisory control, or to the benefits derived from the variety of daily activities. The nature of the prosecuting institution itself, combining as it does the considerable power components of the police and prosecuting establishments and the authority of public morality and social control, draws to it those who desire to act from a position of power. The prosecutor represents the authority-wielding arm of society. By his daily exercise of discretion he critically affects the lives of those whom he is prosecuting. He dispenses sanctions from a position of impersonal power with little risk to himself.

Prosecutors were often explicit about their attraction to the authoritative nature of the position and its power components. One explained how some of the satisfactions of power are acquired: "It is a position of some power and it goes to your head. Like judges, you get used to this power and you never get over it. Everyone is coming to us, asking us 'Can I have a remand?, Can I?, Will you?' People always come to you and want things from you. That kind of power could corrupt. Some prosecutors say, 'This is my court' or 'I run this court.'" Another prosecutor, when asked what satisfactions he gained from the position of prosecutor, replied:

The positive side is sort of a satisfaction in the manipulation of power. You've got to escape from yourself as a person because you are in public life and you have to attempt to be a reasoned, thinking human being and you must attempt to curb your natural emotionalism. I feel I'm a public person and must conduct myself accordingly. It makes me an interesting person at a cocktail party. As long as you are a prosecutor, in your private life you must conduct yourself in the light of that, with respect ...

Another, speaking of the attractions of his position suggested that:

It's the type of job that is easily abused. It can go to your head. You can think that I'm the boss and I'm it. This is part of the reason some of the police don't get along with prosecutors. But it is a long life and you have to keep that in mind. It is the kind of job where you can release suppressed superiority desires. At the outset you mention the name prosecutor and it has a glamorous sound to it. You have a superiority over defence counsel and the police. It either stays with you or you mellow into a diplomat. The job can go to your head and it does influence your social habits. I can't drink now in certain places where I know the hoods hang out.

The psychic satisfactions of power manipulation are undisguised. Whether the position shapes the personality of those engaged in prosecution over the years, or whether it attracts a certain type of individual who accords prestige (either consciously or unconsciously) to the power position enjoyed by the prosecutor, or both, is not easily determined. Alexander and Staub have suggested that prosecuting attorneys may be activated by a set of unconscious, sadistic tendencies "which not only play an important role in the given professional activities but are not infrequently the decisive factors in the matter of choosing a profession ... The endeavour to assure the security of state order permits the attorney to give vent to his unconscious tendency to inflict suffering upon others; his official work keeps the unofficial work of the subconscious unnoticed."[2] This is strong language with which to characterize those who enthusiastically pursue prosecution as a career. At the same time the foregoing analysis is not without some support in

2 See F. Alexander and H. Staub, *The Criminal, the Judge and the Public*, 25 (1956).

the comments made by one experienced prosecutor when asked what type of individual he believed was most attracted to prosecution:

... It attracts more of one type – more neurotics – more people who are not completely integrated in their social relationships, the people who are not particularly sensible and well-adjusted, more isolated types. The violence and dishonesty attracts certain people. It's a world of cunning, unlike the world that they are used to ... Also there is a certain sense of power and it may be a person who feels insecure and not particularly well-adjusted in his social relationships, that the power in court helps to make up for this lack of security outside the courtroom.

4 A DIFFERENT BREED OF LAWYER

Although part of the legal profession, the office of the prosecutor has acquired certain attributes of a subculture which set it apart from the larger professional lawyer culture. The prosecutor has developed skills and sympathies which are part of a segmented interest group within the interstices of the profession as a whole.[3] In some measure, then, prosecutors constitute a group apart from the general legal community with an ethos of their own. The in-group solidarity is not based on similar values supported by the collective activity in which they participate, but is part of the strong interacting relationship between the occupational culture of the prosecutor and the culture of the broader legal community.

The way in which the prosecutor sees the role of the defence lawyer influences his conception of his own role.[4] Turner points out that "Once the actor formulates a conception of the role of the other, the manner in which that conception serves to shape his own behaviour is unaffected by the accuracy or inaccuracy of that conception."[5] Evaluations of the defence lawyer's role and his actions may be made by

3 See Smith, "Contingencies of Professional Differentiation," 63 *Am. J. Soc.* 410–14 (1958); also see Marshall, "The Recent History of Professionalism in Relation to Social Structure and Social Policy," 5 *Can. J. of Econ. & Pol. Sci.* 325 (1939); also "Professions," 92 *Daedalus* (1963).
4 "Role refers to behavior rather than position, so that one may enact a role but cannot occupy a role ... The role is made up of all those norms which are thought to apply to a person occupying a given position." Turner, "Role-taking, Role Standpoint and Reference: Group Behavior," 61 *Am. J. Soc.* 316, at p. 316–17 (1956).
5 *Ibid.*, at p. 318.

the prosecutor by projection rather than from personal knowledge of the other's behaviour.[6] The prosecutor may attribute to defence lawyers emotions, ideas, and attitudes which they do not in fact possess, but which originate in the prosecutor himself. At the same time, the prosecutor may react to the defence lawyer on the basis of prior experience with that particular lawyer or with others assumed to be like him. Turner suggests that "[t]he actor engages in role-taking in order to determine how he ought to act toward the other."[7] Often the prosecutor shapes his own performance according to what he judges to be the probable effect of interaction between his role and the inferred role of the defence lawyer.

Mead has pointed out that the actor in the "game" must have in mind the roles of the other players as illustrated in the following example from baseball:

The skilful player in a game such as baseball cannot act solely according to a set of rules. The first baseman can learn in general when he is to field the ball, when to run to first base, etc. But, in order to play intelligently and to be prepared for less clearly defined incidents in the game, he must adjust his role performance to the roles of the other players. This adjustment is in terms of the effect of interaction among roles to the end of minimizing the score of the opposing team. When the first baseman fields the ball, runs to first, throws to home, etc., will depend upon what he thinks each of the other players will do and how his action will combine most effectively with theirs to keep the score down.[8]

Similarly, the prosecutor does not act according to a set of rules but rather in a manner conditioned by his environment and the actions of the other participants in the prosecuting environment – the police, the defence lawyers, and the judiciary. His actions are reactions to the

6 In the case of projection, one constructs the other role as he would if he himself were in the situation or had made the particular gesture. When role-taking proceeds in this manner, the particular identity of the other is immaterial to the role content, since the role conceptions of the actor are simply imputed to the other: *ibid.*, at p. 319.
7 *Ibid.*, at p. 320.
8 G. H. Mead, *Mind, Self and Society*, 149 (1934). Turner has pointed out that "while role-taking is a process of placing specific behaviors of the other in the context of his total role, the attention of the actor is never equally focused upon all the attitudes implied by that role. Rather, one's orientation determines that only certain attitudes of the other-role will be especially relevant to the determination of his own behavior ... The demands of the actor's role determine the selection of aspects of the other-role for emphasis": *ibid.*, at p. 149.

behaviour of these other players and his responses reflect his best judgment of how the game is to be played in order to keep the adversary's score down.

There is no clear consensus in the prosecutor's office of the function, goals, and standards to be applied in daily professional activities. It is not only that each man interprets his function differently but that there are a number of differing institutional interpretations of the prosecutorial function: the rigid adversarial stance; the managerial, administrative, and supervisory attitude; the independent role as a lawyer subscribing to the profession's general ethics; and the concept of a co-operative conciliator responsive to reciprocal relationships between defence and prosecution. As noted earlier some of the younger members of the prosecutor's office feel closer to police officers and their expediting values than to their professional colleagues, the defence lawyers. This creates an in-group solidarity between prosecutors and police which may be associated with some hostility towards the out-group which is composed of accused persons and the defence lawyers who represent them. Some prosecutors tend to associate the lawyer with his client. Suspicion characterizes their relations with defence lawyers and results in limited responses to defence requests for pre-trial disclosure and compromises.

Others identify with the values of the defence lawyers and accord those values some prestige. This is reflected in the prosecutor's own self-conception, one of being clearly a part of the general legal community, and in his interaction with the defence lawyers. Those who had practiced law before becoming prosecutors accorded some prestige to the role of the defence lawyer, and seemed more sympathetic towards the defence role. This empathy was often reflected in the flexible attitude taken to pre-trial negotiations and to disclosure. These same prosecutors seemed particularly aware of police pressures and imposed conscious limits on police participation in the prosecuting process.

The prosecutor may be regarded by the police as one of them and therefore part of the police subculture, and by defence lawyers as part of the legal fraternity and as such responsive to concepts such as the rule of law and traditional legal norms. It is from this conflicting occupational context that his position gains its meaning and from which career orientations take their shape. In addition, the conflicting concepts conditioned by the demands of the adversarial system and the public image of the prosecutor on the one hand and the administrative demands and the need for informal and flexible relations on the other, contribute to the problem of defining any one dominant set of occupational values subscribed to by all the prosecutors. They, for the most part, rarely verbalize any consideration of the ideals, aspirations, or goals posited by the criminal justice system, but appear to reflect a self-image of men of action who are not contemplative of their professional values and the system within which they play a major role. Customary patterns of action are pursued with a sense of independence from supervisory direction or control.

5 INDEPENDENCE AND ITS LIMITATIONS

Prosecutors generally reject the social and political roles often associated with the extra-professional life of the lawyer and find their own role without these social, political, and client obligations more satisfying. There are no pressures upon him to fulfil any extra-professional role and social, political, or other extra-professional activities play no overt part in the prosecutor's career advancement.[9] This is not the case in most of the United States. "Although ... [the prosecutor] was under relatively little supervision in his daily activities, he had to be careful to stay in the good graces of the United States Attorney who, holding an essentially political position, was very sensitive to the criticism of the press, the judges and the defence bar, all of whom were quick to note the rising number of acquittals."[10]

In the county of York prosecutors feel relatively free from political or administrative controls and exercise independent judgment and responsibility within general policy guidelines. They do not view

9 Contrast the freedom from political interference in the career advancement of the Canadian prosecutor with the situation reported in New York where a district attorney admitted that his assistants were selected for him by his political organization and assigned this fact as a reason why he should not be held to account for the deficiencies of this office. Drukman, "Investigation," 15 *Panel* 13 (1937), See also Wardel and Wood, "The Extra-Professional Role of the Lawyer," 61 *Am. J. Soc.* 304 (1956).
10 Kaplan, "The Prosecutorial Discretion: A Comment," 60 *NW. U. L. Rev.* 174, at p. 184 (1965–6).

themselves as employees subject to the control of their employer. They feel free, as lawyers, to exercise complete discretion within the general organizational structure. One prosecutor suggested that the benefits of this position are considerable: "The beauty is that you are alone on the job and you make your own decisions but at the same time you have other people around to pick their brains if you need to."

At the same time prosecutors cannot be fitted into a legal tradition of individualism comparable to the individual relationship of trust which exists between solicitor and client. There are, to be sure, some resemblances of a client-solicitor relationship present in the prosecutor's position as part-time adviser to the police. But involvement with individual cases and the satisfactions of representing clients who pay fees in recognition of ability are unavailable to him. His satisfaction and the enjoyment of status must be derived from the power and prestige components of his office. If these components no longer represent an adequate source of satisfaction, the absence of personal involvement – whether in successes or failures – seems to result in a loss of personal commitment to the prosecuting process. Dissatisfaction and disengagement may increase over the years until daily duties seem to provide little challenge and the work becomes routine. After a number of years, some prosecutors expressed concern about the repetitive nature of their experience and suggested that the sameness may breed boredom:

I became interested in the work. I could hardly believe I was being paid for it. This attitude lasted for about three years ...

After four or five years it is self-defeating, as in any civil service employment the longer you are employed – it's the law of diminishing returns after a given time. I thought it would start in four or five years. At the end of four or five years I have done everything that it is possible to do and everything from now on would be repetition ... There are guys who after twenty years in this job are using very little brain matter because there is so little that is new or challenging. Persons who are in this office for years are bored to tears ... It's fine for keen people out of law school for two, three, four years, but after that period of time, after that, an attitude can settle in.

Another suggested that the main problem with the position was "boredom emanating from the never ending stream of cases. If you are a defence lawyer you have a personal stake and personal involvement in each case and you're dealing with a human being. Here, as a prosecutor, you don't get that. You get file after file after file, and you try one case after another, day after day. It becomes sort of clinical ..."

6 DETERMINANTS OF PROFESSIONAL PERSPECTIVES

The conflicting functional demands placed upon the prosecutor, the lack of clearly defined institutional goals, and the failure to prepare the novice for the prosecuting practice before he is propelled into the lower court arena, may permanently restrict the horizon of professional perspectives on the part of the young prosecutor and inhibit proper adjustment to his new position. Those with general professional experience gained before their entry into the prosecutor's office seemed more resistant to police values and the temptation to manipulate raw power. They also seemed more able to step back from their day-to-day involvement in the prosecuting environment and, thus detached, better equipped to evaluate their own professional perspectives and those of their colleagues. One sensitive prosecutor, who had spent considerable time in the criminal courts both as a defence lawyer and as a prosecuting attorney, summed up some of the most pressing professional problems:

... You can become desensitized by magistrates' court and the assembly line procedure there and the officers shouting at the accused to keep quiet or to take the gum out of his mouth. This can be very influential on a young fellow when he sees these accused men herded into the dock and pushed together and treated like animals. If a young man is of an authoritarian or jackboot mind, he would think of these people in the docket as something a little sub-human. There are very few like that but it is the volume, the mass of people, and the mass of cases, and the never-ending assembly line that can influence the outlook of a prosecutor. It is a strange system, and it's strange that it works as well as it does, and there isn't more injustice.

CHAPTER SEVEN

Reciprocal Relationships

1 THE TIES THAT BIND

To arrive at an understanding of the dynamics of the legal environment and the prosecuting system the phenomenon of social groupings must be investigated. Social bonds are created within the legal environment by the rendering of a service and the expression of the recipient's gratitude on an appropriate occasion by a return of a service. If the recipient continues to reciprocate for the exchange it indicates a continuing gratitude which serves as an inducement to further exchanges and thus creates a social bond between the two.[1] A sense of trust is required for and promoted by the exchange of services or kindnesses. The continued association in a relation to trust alters the initially isolated position of the individuals involved and groups them into a new social relationship.[2]

It was George Simmel, the sociologist, who said, "All contacts among men rest on the schema of giving and returning the equivalence ... [G]ratitude establishes the bond of interaction, of reciprocity of service and return service, even when they are not guaranteed by external coercion ..."[3] It is this concept of reciprocity and exchange which contributes to an analysis of the fabric of informal relations, obligations, and interaction existing between the prosecutor and the

1 See P. M. Blau, *Exchange and Power in Social Life*, 4 (1964).
2 See E. Durkheim, *Suicide* (G. Simpson, ed., 1951).
3 George Simmel, *The Sociology of George Simmel*, 387 (trans. and ed. Kurt H. Wolff, 1950). See also Simmel, *Conflict and the Web of Group Affiliations* (trans. Kurt H. Wolff and Reinhard Bendix, 1955).

defence lawyer.[4] These relationships and exchanges of services, unlike economic or contractual exchanges, are based on unspecified and unenforceable obligations. Although not "guaranteed by external coercion" the relationships are regulated by, and conform to, internal, interpersonal norms. As Cicero once pointed out: "There is no duty more indispensable than that of returning a kindness ... all men distrust one forgetful of a benefit."[5]

Exchange relations, or relations of trust, evolve as a slow process. A testing period, where little trust is required and little risk is involved, becomes a precondition to reciprocal relationships that are based on proven trustworthiness and a continued feed-back of appreciation.[6] Peter Blau suggests that

by discharging their obligations for services rendered, if only to provide inducements for the supply of more assistance, individuals demonstrate their trustworthiness and the gradual expansion of mutual service is accompanied by a parallel growth of mutual trust. Hence, processes of social exchange, which may originate in pure self-interest, generate trust in social relations through their recurrent and gradually expanding character.[7]

The data in the county of York suggest that the prosecutor and the defence lawyer are bound together within the prosecutorial environment by a variety of informal relations; the relationship grew unless preconceptions and barriers had been formed by prior associations or reputation. The element of bargaining for the valuable sought in the exchange becomes part of the reciprocal process. The prosecutor may view the impending exchange with some suspicion and may hesitate to part with his valuable until he has gained his objective. For example,

4 George C. Homans, *Social Behavior*, 13 (1961). Homans has developed this theory in his "Social Behavior as Exchange," 63 *Am. J. Soc.* 597 (1958). A number of scholars have commented on the importance of this theory: Claude Lévi-Strauss, *Les structures élémentaires de la parenté* (1949); Raymond Firth, *Primitive Polynesian Economy* (1950); Emile Durkheim, *Suicide*; Marcel Mauss, *The Gift* (trans. Ian Cunnison, 1954); B. Malinowski, *Crime and Custom in Savage Society* (1932). Most recently the concept of reciprocity has been developed by Blau, *Exchange and Power*; Howard Becker, *Man in Reciprocity* (1956); and in a cogent paper by A. W. Gouldner, "*The Norm of Reciprocity*: A Preliminary Statement," 65 *Am. J. Soc.* 161 (1960).
5 Quoted by Gouldner, *supra*, at p. 161.
6 This feed-back may be in terms of favours, but excessive reciprocation at an early stage may prove embarrassing and limit the future relationship. See Blau, *Exchange and Power*, at p. 94.
7 *Ibid.*, at p. 94.

it is the practice for the prosecution, when withdrawing charges or when accepting a plea to a lesser charge or an included offence, to arraign the accused on the charge or charges which it was agreed would proceed; only when the guilty plea has been recorded by the court will the prosecutor inform the presiding judge that he is not proceeding on the other offences.

2 THE POWER TO DISCLOSE

In addition to the negotiated plea of guilty, a helpful exchange which is influenced by the quality of prosecutor-defence reciprocal relations relates to the pre-trial disclosure of the prosecution's case against the accused. Legislative provisions in Canada do not require complete disclosure by the prosecution of its case before trial.[8] There is no specific code provision permitting the defence to inspect written statements made to the police by prosecution witnesses.[9] There is no duty placed upon the police or prosecution to open their files to an accused or to his defence lawyer.[10]

The statement of W. B. Common, QC, former director of public prosecutions for Ontario, is often put forward as a definitive declaration of prosecuting practice relating to disclosure:[11]

8 An accused is entitled, after he has been committed for trial or at his trial, to inspect the indictment, his own statement, the evidence and exhibits, if any: C.C. s. 512. S. 512(6) also provides that the "trial shall not be postponed to enable the accused to secure copies unless the court is satisfied that the failure of the accused to secure them before the trial is not attributable to lack of diligence on the part of the accused."

9 See s. 10(1) of the Canada Evidence Act, R.S.C. 1952, c. 307. It provides as follows: "Upon any trial a witness may be cross-examined as to previous statements made by him in writing, or reduced to writing, relative to the subject-matter of the case, without such writing being shown to him; but if it is intended to contradict the witness by the writing, his attention must, before such contradictory proof can be given, be called to those parts of the writing that are to be used for the purpose of so contradicting him; the judge, at any time during the trial, may require the production of the writing for his inspection, and thereupon make such use of it for the purpose of the trial as he thinks fit." In *R.* v. *Lepine* (1962), 39 W.W.R.(n.s.) 253, 38 C.R. 145 (Sask.) production was ordered of a memorandum prepared by a police officer and referred to by him just before trial.

10 See *R.* v. *Silvester and Trapp* (1959), 29 W.W.R.(n.s.) 361, 31 C.R. 190 (B.C.).

11 In *R.* v. *Finland* (1959–60), 31 C.R. 364, the court held that the Criminal Code did not require the production for inspection before trial by the accused or his counsel of written statements of Crown witnesses obtained by the police. The court

... in all criminal cases there is complete disclosure by the prosecution of its case to the defence. To use a colloquialism, there are no "fast ones" pulled by the Crown. The defence does not have to disclose its case to the Crown. We do not ask it for a complete and full disclosure of the case. If there are statements by witnesses, statements of accused ... they know exactly what our case is, and there is nothing hidden or kept back or suppressed so that the accused person is taken by surprise at a trial by springing a surprise witness on him. In other words, I again emphasize the fact that every safeguard is provided by the Crown to ensure that an accused person, not only in capital cases but in every case, receives and is assured of a fair and legal trial.[12]

The interview data do not support Mr Common's description of prosecuting practice. The production of statements of Crown witnesses for inspection by the defence before trial is a matter solely within the discretion of the prosecutor. That discretion is exercised when he decides whether to disclose information to the defence beyond the minimal disclosure required by law. On what factors or criteria does the prosecutor base his decision to disclose or not to disclose? The following interviews suggest that the quality of the reciprocal relationships between prosecutors and defence are the determining factor in the prosecutor's exercise of discretion with respect to pre-trial disclosure. A senior prosecutor enumerates some of the considerations which influence his decision:

Those I can trust I can communicate with, and those I can't, I won't give more than the law requires me to – which isn't very much. Some practitioners have no scruples in the practice of criminal law. Some are plain dishonest and under the guise of acting in the interests of the client they can be very dishonest. You learn who you can trust. I start out with the premise that I give no more than the law requires me to. I relax that depending on the man I am talking to. If it was a person like ... x ... I could hand him my brief. I don't say, as some people do, that there is full disclosure by the prosecution, and I withhold some of that disclosure from those I can't trust. I start out saying that I will give them what the law requires me to and then from there it is *ex gratia* assistance to those I can trust ...

also ruled that both *R*. v. *Mahadeo*, [1936] 3 w.w.r. 443; [1936] 2 All e.r. 813, and *R*. v. *Clarke* (1930), 22 Cr. App. r. 58 were authority for the proposition that statements must be produced, if required, at the trial and not before.
12 Reported in the Special Lectures of the Law Society of Upper Canada (1955), at p. 3. In *R*. v. *Lantos*, [1964] 2 c.c.c. 52 the bc Court of Appeal ruled that statements of prospective Crown witnesses do not constitute "evidence" which an accused is entitled to examine before trial.

Of course, there are other factors that govern. A man who begins as a counsel in a criminal case may not be the accused's counsel tomorrow. It's not like in a civil case where he would appear on the record and would have to bring a motion to remove himself from the record. In England, between the barrister and the accused, there is a buffer. The barrister seldom sees the accused and the witnesses. Here the lawyer has intimate contact with the accused. If I disclose to defence counsel what the Crown's case is, he may sit down with the accused, in jail or even more dangerous in his office, and tell him the case and the next thing you know someone has gone to see your material witnesses ...

... But the manner in which he comes to see me may be important. He may say "Will you consider this?" – in a dispassionate way. But if somebody belabours me and tells me what I should do, I'm not going to give him much in return. He's asking for a favour and when you ask for a favour you don't bludgeon someone into doing you a favour. ...

... Very often the honest ones, if they know the full story, will plead their client guilty. If the Crown hedges and won't tell them what they are going to face they will plead not guilty. If it is a lawyer that you do not trust you will not appraise him fully of the Crown's case. He is going to plead not guilty in any case and he will use the information, given in confidence by the Crown, in preparing his own defence. I have had a lawyer that I showed a dope sheet to use the information in the dope sheet in cross-examination, and he cross-examined the Crown witness on the dope sheet by saying, "You are saying this now and you didn't say it before." Now that lawyer will never see any Crown evidence again. Generally speaking, I don't let lawyers see the dope sheet. Ninety per cent of the time if a lawyer asks what the case is, I will read the salient facts from the dope sheet – maybe he will decide to plead guilty.

The foregoing suggests that the prosecutor views pre-trial disclosure, pleas to lesser charges, and the withdrawal of charges as favours to be exchanged with certain defence lawyers. These favours will not be available to defence counsel who are abrasive or demanding, but will be available to those who have proven themselves part of the trustworthy social grouping. A defence lawyer who is part of the reciprocating environment, who is "trusted," who is "safe," will obtain full disclosure of the prosecution's case before trial. He is "safe" if he does not utilize the evidence obtained in pre-trial disclosure for cross-examination of prosecution witnesses and is likely to enter a guilty plea after an assessment of the prosecution's evidentiary strength. The entry of a proportionate number of guilty pleas by defence counsel is a prerequisite. Defence counsel who consistently take an adversarial position or regularly enter not guilty pleas on behalf of their clients will not share in the benefits of pre-trial disclosure. A comment on reciprocity, in another context, seems to confirm the necessity for mutuality in the relationship: "Unlike ordinary price discrimination reciprocity results in lower prices only to those customers who happen also to be suppliers."[13]

3 THE OUTSIDER

The failure on the part of the defence lawyer to reciprocate by entering a proportionate number of guilty pleas results in loss of trust and, ultimately, in exclusion from further exchanges and an immediate decline in his social status among the prosecutors: "A few want to look at the dope sheet and say that they will plead guilty. Often once they have seen it and they see the Crown's evidence isn't as strong as they thought it was, they decide to plead not guilty." Similarly, if a defence lawyer fails to discharge an obligation, for example, if he utilizes prosecution evidence disclosed to him in confidence for purposes of cross-examination, the exchange relationship will be terminated. If the defence lawyer does not personally participate in returning services as an expression of gratitude, the reciprocal relationship will not survive:

Certain defence counsel will come into your office and say, "Good morning, lovely day," and then will go out and see their client and say to their client, "I've just paid off the prosecution and that will be another two hundred dollars." These same defence lawyers will do the same thing with a magistrate. They'll go in to see him, say, "Good morning," walk out, and tell their client that they've just spoken to the magistrate and they require another two hundred dollars ...

Another example of defence behaviour which will result in loss of trust and exclusion from reciprocal exchanges is related by another prosecutor:

You have a case for trial. It's set peremptory and you find out that the defence has called the witnesses and told them that the case is not proceeding and

13 See Hale and Hale, "Reciprocity under the Antitrust Laws: A Comment," 113 *U. of Pa. L. Rev.* 69, at p. 75 (1964–5).

that they don't have to show up in court the next day. Then he gets up in court the next day and says that he is ready to proceed and that he has not been notified that the Crown is going to ask for a delay. Some lawyers put on five cases in one day so that they can only go on with one and so that the others have to be put over. The more times the Crown witnesses come to court the more the Crown witnesses get fed up ...

Some prosecutors were particularly suspicious of defence motives. "There are about ten I trust at the most." Another said that he does not engage in any informality with defence lawyers and, in fact, confronts them directly.

A lawyer who is not considered safe or trustworthy and excluded from the reciprocal exchange relationship may be subjected to differential treatment.

If I don't like a certain defence lawyer I can hold his case up by keeping it at the end of the list for two or three days. Or I can decide not to disclose anything to him. It depends on what I think of the defence, how much I will disclose to him. If I trust him, so he won't use the evidence to bring perjured evidence against the prosecution. I will disclose to him.

Lawyers who are engaged in the defence of criminal prosecutions are categorized by prosecutors as those who are absolutely trustworthy, safe, and therefore part of the reciprocal exchange relationship; those who fall into a grey area but who are, for the most part, trustworthy; those who are, for the most part, untrustworthy; and those completely excluded from the reciprocal exchange relationship. A prosecutor admitted that his personal feelings towards particular defence counsel were reflected in the extent of his pre-trial disclosure to them:

In the first category, lawyers I trust absolutely, I give them the fullest and frankest disclosure at the earliest possible moment. I would do the same thing with a young lawyer if he asked me; I would be co-operative and helpful. With "bar rattlers" I would stick to the law and they would obtain no disclosure until after the preliminary hearing. With ... y ... and others like him, I may let my emotions run away with me and try to obstruct him.

The defence lawyer, then, has much to gain in establishing a relationship of trust with the prosecutor for it may result in an expanding horizon of pre-trial alternatives for his clients and open up exits from the system before formal trial procedures are begun. On the other hand, if reciprocal relationships of trust are not established the defence lawyer and his client may suffer substantially different treatment. For the prosecutor, reciprocal exchanges are not only a time-saving device but create a co-operative atmosphere, not so much of success as of minimizing loss. The prosecutor loses less often in the open and formal forum and is able to process a large number of cases to an expedient determination. Negotiation at the pre-trial stage, and the number of alternatives available to an accused and his counsel, may depend as much on the quality of the relationship between prosecutor and defence as upon the expediting procedures based on administrative values.

4 REINS OF POWER

Exchange processes within the legal environment give rise to a differentiation of power. "A person who commands services others need, and who is independent of any at their command, attains power over others by making the satisfaction of their need contingent on their compliance."[14] It is the defence lawyer who most often requests the services of the prosecution in reciprocal exchanges and correspondingly pays the cost in the subordination involved in expressing the request and manifesting gratitude for the exchange. As one prosecutor said:

A lot depends on the approach of counsel. If they're polite with me, then I am polite with them. If it will help to get us a guilty plea, I will give it to him. If it is doubtful, maybe the guy shouldn't have been arrested in the first place. But a lot depends on the approach of counsel ... just as people are different, so are defence counsel, and if I have a good relationship with him, and I do with most of them, then I disclose everything.

In requesting the "favour" the defence lawyer rewards the prosecutor with some prestige and power in the relationship.[15]

14 Blau, *Exchange and Power*, at p. 22. Power is defined by Max Weber as the "probability that one actor within a social relationship will be in a position to carry out his own will despite resistance": M. Weber, *The Theory of Social and Economic Organization* (1950). Tawney similarly defines power: "Power may be defined as the capacity of an individual, or group of individuals, to modify the conduct of other individuals, or groups, in the manner which he desires, and to prevent his own conduct being modified in the manner in which he does not": R. H. Tawney, *Equality*, 229 (1933).

15 Blau, *Exchange and Power*, at p. 108. See also the discussion in Homans, *Social Behavior*, at pp. 318–19, and Mauss, *The Gift*, at pp. 10–11, 39–40. Emerson has presented a schema for examining "power dependence": Richard M. Emerson, "Power Dependence Relations," 27 *Am. Soc. Rev.* 31, at p. 41 (1962).

Some prosecutors appear indifferent to the exchange process and in being so modify the process so to increase their position of power. The prosecutor's refusal to participate in the reciprocal relationships may imply his lack of respect for a particular defence lawyer or for defence lawyers generally and that he considers them unworthy of being his companions in an exchange. The attitude, "I don't like mixing with defence lawyers," and the refusal to participate, leads to rigid and sometimes hostile social relationships.

5 A MINORITY FOR TRIAL

Prosecutors establish reciprocal relationships with those who are able to reciprocate, resulting in the neglect of those who are unable to do so. Reciprocity is largely confined to those defence lawyers who have been admitted to the social circle, dependent as it is on the quality of their relationship with the prosecutor. Reciprocity results in discrimination, for benefits are limted to those lawyers who happen to be suppliers of benefits. Lawyers who do not supply their "quota" of guilty pleas and contest every case are subjected to "the bare bones of the legal system." The unrepresented accused has no opportunity to engage in pre-trial reciprocal exchanges.

Reciprocity standing alone constitutes a violation of the rule of law and the principle of equality before the law. It tends to create an exchange atmosphere outside normal court procedures, an atmosphere which is anti-adversarial and discourages participation in the trial process. Attempts to limit this reciprocal exchange may be as unsuccessful in the legal environment as in commercial markets:

It is, of course, obvious that preventing reciprocity, like attacking any practice, reaches only the symptoms and does not eliminate the disease. As we have seen reciprocity is possible only if markets are impure or imperfect. Reduction of impurities, may be too expensive. If the impurities, for example, are rooted in a minimum scale of production so that their elimination would involve inefficiency ... [16]

Where the striving for the realization of expediting administrative

16 For a criticism of reciprocity in a commercial law context, see Hale and Hale, "Reciprocity"; and Phillips, "Reciprocity under the Antitrust Laws: Observations on the Hales' Comment," 113 *U. of Pa. L. Rev.* 77 (1964).

values combines with strong reciprocal relationships the substantive decision-making process takes place before trial. In that event, the courtroom forum merely serves a ratifying function and the players mouth words in a ceremony without real significance for the accused. The result is known before trial either as a result of pre-trial prosecutor-defence agreement or prosecutor-defence-judicial agreement. The classic adversarial conflict is becoming less a part of the day-to-day functioning of the criminal justice system in North America. That is not to say that adversarial clashes at trial do not often take place, but that for the vast majority of those accused of crimes pure adversarial combat remains a last resort.[17]

Who is it, then, who enters the strictly adversarial forum where charges are pressed as originally laid, where the trial takes place, and the accused is convicted or acquitted of the charge as originally specified? For the accused who has no intention of entering a guilty plea to the offence charged or any other offence there is little to be gained from entering into pre-trial negotiations. Without the prospect of a guilty plea the reciprocal pre-trial exchanges are of little value and may in fact inhibit adversarial advantages. The unrepresented accused may enter the adversarial forum because of his inexperience and unawareness that an exchange system is available. The negotiators whose pre-trial negotiations have been unsuccessful may be forced to trial. It may be the fledgling lawyer who wishes to hone his rapier on the prosecution. It may be the lawyer from one jurisdiction who is representing a client in another, which is as a matter of administration non-expediting, who is not usually accepted as a welcome participant in that local reciprocating environment. It may be that the case is one that has gained such public notoriety that compromise is impossible. Or it may be that the accused is represented by a lawyer who acts for his client in the belief that it is the adversarial forum, with the protections it provides, that best insures the rights of the accused and a fair determination of the charges against him.

17 The introduction in the province of Ontario of a new scheme of legal aid may increase the number of cases which proceed to trial as the fees paid to lawyers by the provincial government are determined by the time spent on the case, particularly in court. Whether the provisions of the Ontario scheme will result in an increased resort to courtroom conflict must be the subject of another inquiry. See The Legal Aid Act, 1966, c. 80 (Ont.), amended by An Act to Amend The Legal Aid Act, Bill 124, session 1968–69.

This lawyer might be characterized by his colleagues as a "big gambler" for if he wins at trial his client is acquitted and is totally freed from the system. If he loses, he loses completely and on conviction the full sanctions of the court are applied to his client. The majority of defence counsel, however, avoid battle, shun confrontation, and avoid the big gamble of complete acquittal or total conviction. Instead, they negotiate a settlement more or less acceptable to both the representatives of the state and to the accused. The criteria on which the settlement is based, much like the agreements themselves, continue as part of a little known jurisprudence.

CHAPTER EIGHT

Conflict and Compromise

1 THE ADVERSARY SYSTEM

Common law criminal procedure is founded on the adversary system and it is accusatorial. As such, it is based on the belief that the truth will emerge from the struggle between the two contesting parties where each presents its case before an impartial tribunal. It was Lord Eldon who said in a notable passage that "truth is best discovered by powerful statements on both sides of the question."[1] Counsel on each side will do his best to establish his client's and to destroy his opponent's case. Out of this conflict truth and justice will emerge. The accused must know the specific nature of the charge. He must be confronted by the witnesses against him and he may be convicted only if the evidence proves, beyond a reasonable doubt, that he committed the specific crime with which he has been charged. The trial process encourages each side to maintain polar positions and a combative or at least competitive spirit. One side will win and the other will lose. In this all or nothing engagement there is a certain sweet simplicity of result. It is either good or bad – a result that perpetuates certainty and symmetry, that supports the generality of the principles while avoiding any tendency toward particularization in decision-making or toward flexibility in reaching solutions. The officially maintained certainty militates against any compromise which may threaten confidence in the established rules and moral firmness; such confidence and certitude are considered necessary by those who are fearful that any solution other

1 See *Ex parte Lloyd* (1822), Mont. 70, n.

than an absolute one may be a sign of moral ambivalence. The quest for security and certainty in rules is best supported by the "win-or-lose" outcome which characterizes the adversary system.

If the adversary system is to work, the two combatants must be kept equal or at least relatively equal. If one is much stronger than the other the superior side will gain a substantial advantage and thus undermine a proper determination. For in that event, true conflict is minimized and the outcome is determined simply by superior power. Hence, the proper functioning of the defence is as vital to the adversary system as the prosecuting and judicial functions. If the accused faces the state's prosecuting structure without benefit of advice or assistance of counsel, or such advice or assistance is delayed, the right to challenge the prosecution, which is indispensable to the operation of the adversary system, is gravely impaired.[2]

2 THE PROSECUTOR AS A MINISTER OF JUSTICE

This contest is tempered somewhat by the judicially endorsed concept of the prosecutor, thought of not primarily as a partisan strong-arm of the state but as a "quasi-judicial" officer of the court. The courts have suggested that he should conduct the prosecution in a manner which assists the court and places the case fairly before the jury and nothing more.[3] Prosecutors should avoid inflammatory addresses to the jury or appeals to emotion, and should not advance arguments unwarranted by the evidence.[4] Judicial pronouncements

2 See generally, Grosman, "The Right to Counsel in Canada," 10 *Can. Bar J.* 189 (1967), for a discussion of the limits of adversarial protections in Canada.

3 See H. E. Taschereau, *Criminal Statute Law of the Dominion of Canada*, 841 (2nd ed., 1888); see also *R. v. Murray and Mahoney* (No. 2), [1917] 1 W.W.R. 404, 10 (Alta.) L.R. 275, 27 C.C.C. 247, 33 D.L.R. 702 (C.A.). Sargeant Talfourd, in Dickinsons's Quarter Sessions, says, at p. 495 "... [Crown counsel] should refrain from indulging in invective, and from appealing to the prejudices or passions of the jury; for it is neither in good taste nor right feeling to struggle for a conviction as an advocate in a civil cause contends for a verdict": quoted in Taschereau, *supra*, at p 840.

4 See, e.g., *R. v. Seabrooke*, [1932] O.R. 575, 58 C.C.C. 323, [1932] 4 D.L.R. 116 (C.A.); *R. v. American News Co.*, [1957] O.R. 145, 25 C.R. 374, 118 C.C.C. 152 (C.A.); *R. v. McDonald* (No. 1) 27 C.R. 333, [1958] O.R. 413 (C.A.); and *Tremblay v. R.* (1963), 40 C.R. 303 (Que. C.A.) where, on appeal on a conviction of rape, a new trial was ordered partly on the ground that Crown counsel used inflammatory language. When addressing the jury concerning the noises allegedly

upon the role of the prosecutor have ascribed to him an ethical burden over and above that of the "ordinary" lawyer. "The vocation of an advocate who is prosecuting a criminal is to be in the strictest sense a minister of justice. His duty is to see that every piece of evidence relevant and admissible is presented in due order, without fear and without favour.[5] A senior prosecutor supports this greater ethical burden in a recent publication:

The position of the Crown Attorney is not that of ordinary counsel in a civil case; he is acting in a quasi-judicial capacity or as a minister of justice and ought to regard himself as part of the court rather than as an advocate. He is not to struggle for a conviction nor be betrayed by feelings of professional rivalry to regard the question and issue as one of professional superiority and a contest of skill and pre-eminence.[6]

It is asserted, then, that the role of the prosecutor is one which excludes any notion of winning or losing.[7] He is not to press for a conviction but is to lay all the facts both for and against the accused before the jury.[8] Mr Christmas Humphreys, senior prosecuting counsel at the Old Bailey, in an address entitled "The Duties and Responsibilities of Prosecuting Counsel," adhered to this concept of the prosecuting counsel:

Not only are the defence entitled to call upon the prosecution to assist them to find witnesses and bring them forth or even to make wide inquiry for certain evidence believed to exist, and to spend public money in the cause of

made by the accused the Crown Attorney expressed himself as follows: "On parlait ... des 'grognements' d'un animal. Imaginez la scène : imaginez comment grogne un homme qui a dépassé les limites, – si c'est la vérité, – qui a dépassé les limites de la décence, les limites de la retenue. Et j'irai plus, messieurs : grognements d'un animal, je me demande si l'expression est juste parce qu'il est des actes que les animaux eux-mêmes ne font pas, et qui – si elle a dit la vérité sous serment, – ont été faits par Tremblay, l'accusé. Il est des choses que l'animal n'est pas même assez méchant, mauvais ou vicieux pour faire, parce qu'il n'a pas l'intelligence." See also *McFarland* v. *United States* 150 F.2d. 593 (D.C. Cir. 1945) (in rape case prosecutor kept victim's bloodstained clothing on display); *Simmons* v. *State* 14 Ala. App. 103, 71 So. 979 (1916) (remark calculated to arouse racial prejudice); *Thomas* v. *State* 107 Ark. 469, 155 s.w. 1165 (1913).
5 From an address by Sir John Simon to the Canadian Bar Association reported in 25 *L.N.* 228, at p. 231 (1922).
6 Bull, "The Career Prosecutor of Canada," 53 *J. Crim. L.C.&P.S.* 95 (1962).
7 *Boucher* v. *R.*, [1955] s.c.r. 16, 21, 24.
8 Devlin, *The Criminal Prosecution in England* (1958), at p. 27.

that inquiry, but I believe it to be the duty of prosecuting counsel to offer that aid. And why? Because the prosecutor is at all times a minister of justice though seldom so described. It is not the duty of prosecuting counsel to secure a conviction, nor should any prosecutor ever feel pride or satisfaction in the mere fact of success. Still less should he boast of the percentage of convictions received over a period. The duty of the prosecutor ... is to present to the tribunal a precisely formulated case for the Crown against the accused and to call evidence in support of it. If a defence is raised incompatible with his case, he will cross-examine, dispassionately and with perfect fairness, the evidence so called, and then address the tribunal in reply if he has the right, to suggest that his case is proved. It is no rebuff to his prestige if he fails to convince the tribunal of the prisoner's guilt. His attitude should be so objective that he is, so far as humanly possible, indifferent to the result.[9]

If the adversary system culminates in a trial that pits the skills of one lawyer against another, is it not more realistic to assume that this clash will result in spirited debate? Is there not also that fighting spirit present which drives a man to seek success in combat and victory for his team? Are these motives not engendered by the adversary system and is it not psychologically unlikely that this spirit will disappear in the courtroom?

A prosecutor suggested that the "quasi-judicial," "minister of justice" role is not one which is easily accommodated to an adversarial forum:

There is a danger here that you end up fighting the other lawyer rather than bringing out the facts of the case. With a permanent prosecutor there is a danger of asserting yourself against the defence. The prosecutor is trapped in this adversary system and it becomes for many the most important thing of all. He might use tactics that he might not otherwise use – in the heat of the adversary system. It may be unfair to the accused but the accused fades into the background of the fight between lawyers.

3 CONFLICT RESOLUTION

The question is whether the adversarial stance with its polarities breeds competition in an aggressive sense which in turn begets more competition, or whether the frustrations of competitive confrontation

9 Humphreys, "The Duties and Responsibilities of Prosecuting Counsel," *Crim. L. Rev.* 739 (1955).

lead to communication and then to the establishment of a substantial body of ties between the conflicting parties.

The conflict, depending on its source, may itself tend to encourage mechanisms for conflict resolution. The adjustment of conflict is dependent on the immediate goals or values of the parties to that conflict. There are are two types of basic conflict, conflict of interest and conflict of values.[10] Where there is a conflict of interest the type of social interaction is such that solutions may be reached by an interaction which seems competitive, but since the parties are not morally involved in the result the interests are in fact not diametrically opposed. Where there is only a conflict of interest and the conflicting parties frequently associate with one another integration is increased by the interaction itself. This interaction is stimulated by the realization on the part of the adversaries that common needs and goals may be secured by minimizing the conflict and thereby minimizing the likelihood of maximal loss on either side.

Conflict which is merely a difference of interest and not a clash of values is illustrated by the reaction of a prosecutor who suggested: "You can't identify yourself with each case and you can't identify yourself with each accused. You've got to keep a detached view of the whole thing." Another said: "You try not to get worked up about the case ... You can't get emotionally involved or you would go squirrely." Both parties usually realize that, after all, their interests are not diametrically opposed and that they can both gain more by engaging in some mode of co-operation than by conflict.

At the same time, prosecutors engaged not in a conflict of interest, but of values, tend more often to reject compromise. For although they are continually in contact with defence counsel that contact is limited for the most part to the courtroom, and there is no sharing of values or goals which might tend to bring the two parties together. Instead there is a profound clash of values which not only isolates them but keeps them apart. Conflicts of value, then, cannot be avoided in the same way as conflicts of interest. As Aubert suggests, where there is a conflict of values the terms of exchange are minimal and a scent of the illicit pervades such dealings, for "one cannot trade in values ...

10 See Aubert, "Competition and Dissensus: Two Types of Conflict in Conflict Resolution," 7 *J. Conflict Resolution* 26 (1963).

this illicit nature of compromise on the level of values ... makes it hard to discuss matters quite candidly, thereby decreasing the chances of reaching a solution."[11]

A few prosecutors were unwilling to compromise what appeared to them to represent "the truth" and accordingly demonstrated clearly a conflict of values with defence lawyers.

What burns me is the lawyers who try to settle these cases in chambers with me. Like these dangerous driving cases where you get these inexperienced lawyers who come up to you and say, "Let him go, he'll plead guilty to a lesser charge." To hell with them. If I do something, the lawyers will say, "Look how I got the prosecutor" and they'll charge their clients for it.

Another prosecutor clearly avoided social contact with defence lawyers and espoused an antagonistic attitude toward them: "... I don't like mixing with defence lawyers – they're not buying me meals for the charm of my company ... most civil rights lawyers have little contact with reality and with criminal courts. I guess they're in it because it's good publicity." This represents the attitude of a small minority who assume an adversarial stance, not only in the courtroom, but in pre-trial and even in social relations with defence lawyers. Where there is a substantial conflict of values the defence lawyer may engage in attempts to avoid that particular prosecutor in pre-trial negotiations and at the trial itself. These few prosecutors take particularly rigid attitudes to defence requests for adjournments and to enter pleas to lesser offences. "I don't back down from them. I go into magistrates court and as soon as some defence lawyers see me they want a remand ... You know far more than most defence counsel except that they have a more ingratiating personality."

Only three of the prosecutors interviewed displayed such pschological impediments to compromise.[12] These men were punitive and condescending, insensitive to interpersonal relationships, and prone to attribute their own ideas to others. They appeared to tolerate no ambiguities and no equivocations and seemed to view their rigid attitude as evidence of their toughness and masculinity. For the majority, opposing interests were more easily adjusted.

11 Aubert, "Competition and Dissensus," at p. 29.
12 These prosecutors appeared authoritarian in personality. See *The Authoritarian Personality* (Richard Christie and Marie Jahoda, eds., 1954), and T. W. Adorno, *et al.*, *The Authoritarian Personality* (1950).

The "winner-take-all" legal solution and the adversary theory of conflict is undermined when there is a possibility of mutual gain through co-operation. Co-operation is not completely antithetical to the prosecutor's official position. The judicially endorsed concept of the prosecutor as a quasi-judicial officer of the court and as a minister of justice, lends credence to his non-adversarial activities and to some extent supports the practice of prosecutor-defence co-operation.

4 BARGAINING GAMES

New social investigatory techniques are being developed which may be usefully applied to analyse this critical area of prosecutor-defence interaction. "Game theory" and related tools of social investigation developed by Thomas Schelling[13] and others[14] synthesize social problems and analyse behaviour in terms of identifiable responses of individuals to conflict situations. One of the fundamental distinctions made by the game theory is between "zero-sum" games and "non-zero-sum" games. If there are two parties or players in a zero-sum game, what one party or player wins, the other loses. Thus, after each game played or trial held, one of the party's result or "pay-off" is always zero. This model represents the results obtainable in a criminal trial, for if the prosecution wins the defence must lose and vice versa. In what are called non-zero-sum games there is not this kind of all or nothing constraint on the players. Both players may gain, both players may lose, or one may gain and the other lose and their losses and gains need not necessarily be in equal amounts. Non-zero-sum games are often referred to as "bargaining games" and possess some of the characteristics which are generally considered to be features of bargaining situations, in which conflict of interest and the possibility of mutual gain by co-operation coexist.[15]

13 See generally, on game theory applied to problems of international conflict, T. C. Schelling, *The Strategy of Conflict* (1966), and T. C. Schelling, *Arms and Influence* (1966).
14 See A. Rapoport, *Strategy and Conscience* (1964), and also his *Fights, Games and Debates* (1960); R. D. Luce and H. Raiffa, *Games and Decisions* (1967); *Game Theory and Related Approaches to Social Behavior* (M. Shubik, ed., 1964).
15 See Joseph Willis, "Bargaining Behaviour. I. 'Prominence' as a predictor of the outcome of games of agreement," 3 *J. Conflict Resolution* 102 (1959). See also

These co-operative bargaining situations are most likely to form between prosecutors and defence lawyers where better or more consistent results will be achieved as the outcome of agreement, rather than from a pure adversarial engagement. The extent to which the prosecutor and defence interact will depend on how the outcomes or benefits available through the co-operative relationship compare with those obtainable outside the relationship as a result of the trial process. As was pointed out in the preceding chapter once the attitudes and interests of the prosecutor and the defence lawyer become more mutually favourable, communication and alternatives increase. The initial stage of mild hostility may be preserved by the prosecutor's characterization of the defence lawyer as untrustworthy or by the defence lawyer's competitive action once co-operation by the prosecutor has been extended. Individual differences in personality between those, for example, who are highly competitive and desire victory at all costs, and those who are psychologically hostile, may limit co-operative relationships. But these barriers are, for the most part, the product of extreme value conflict. Once there is positive motivation, encouraged by the nature of the rewards available which lessen the risk or cost involved, the co-operative relationship will be acknowledged by the parties as a more satisfactory adjustment.

Reciprocal or co-operative relations, for the defence lawyer, provide his best alternative; they will secure for him the most favourable continuing results of any of the alternatives available to him including the state of classic adversarial confrontation. For a continued reciprocal relationship between the prosecutor and the defence lawyer means that the latter can more easily arrange for adjournments and can expect to receive a favourable hearing on proposed reductions by the entry of pleas of guilty to lesser offences. Because he will obtain complete disclosure of the prosecution's case he can accurately evaluate his chances at trial and expedite the disposition of cases without useless wrangling

J. E. Coons, "Approaches to Court Imposed Compromise: The Uses of Doubt and Reason," 58 *Nw. L. Rev.* 750, at p. 790 (1963–4); Northrop, "The Mediational Approval Theory of Law in American Legal Realism," 44 Va. *L. Rev.* 347 (1958). See also the importance of mediation in Chinese law: Lubman, "Mao and Mediation: Politics and Dispute Resolution in Communist China," 55 *Calif. L. Rev.* 1284 (1967); Cohen, "Chinese Mediation on the Eve of Modernization," 54 *Calif. L. Rev.* 1201 (1966).

and the risk of loss in the courtroom. His reward is time and money saved. The prosecutor for his part achieves outcomes which are generally much better than those which he could hope to achieve if he went to trial. From his point of view, the ability to keep the process well managed and flowing is more beneficial than engaging in numerous trials with the risk of loss of convictions and time.

Thibault and Kelley suggest that these relationships develop as a result of the relative power or "expertness" of one of the parties to the relationship and the need of the other to rely on the other's "expertise." The prosecutor's discretionary decision to disclose or not to disclose his case to the defence counsel before trial is one example of his special expertise or power.

One person can improve the outcomes of another in one or both of two ways: by providing him with rewards or by reducing his costs. A special case of the ability to cut another person's costs is exemplified by the 'expert', an individual who has special knowledge he can impart to others which enables them to perform rewarding activities with less effort, less anxiety, or in less time – in general, at lower cost.[16]

This statement is applicable to the present prosecutor-defence relationship and the current limits placed on pre-trial disclosure by the exercise of the prosecutor's discretion. On the other hand, compulsory pre-trial disclosure by the prosecutor would significantly alter the relationship.

If the receiver of expert advice (the defence lawyer) "becomes enabled to provide himself with such information ... the expert's power is lost. It is as if he had a cost-cutting tool which he gives the other person. Only if he retains ownership of the tool and can withdraw it at any time does he continue to derive power from it."[17] If the prosecutor thus loses his expertness or power to give benefits that cannot be obtained otherwise the relationship is no longer necessary.

There are, then, under the present practice where the prosecutor controls pre-trial disclosure and alternatives, positive attractions for both parties to the compromises available by engaging in the reciprocal relationship. For the prosecutor can supply benefits to the defence with little cost to himself. As long as the defence conforms to the ethics

16 J. W. Thibault and H. H. Kelley, *The Social Psychology of Groups*, 109 (1959).
17 *Idem.*

of the reciprocal relationship the prosecutor will augment benefits to the defence as a reward for compliance. As long as the defence counsel manifests his adherence to the reciprocal ethics by not cross-examining Crown witnesses on evidence disclosed to him in confidence by the prosecutor and by the entry of an appropriate number of guilty pleas, he will continue to receive the rewards inherent in this exchange.

Loss of rewards is implicitly threatened by the prosecutor for non-compliance or for aggressive competitive behaviour which is seen as a misuse of the prosecutor's trust. Defence counsel learns quickly to augment his rewards by behaving in a certain way rather than in another since conformity by the defence to the reciprocal requirements means concrete gains with respect to pre-trial disclosure and flexible dispositional alternatives. When defence counsel does not conform he adds to his own cost of obtaining results as he encounters prosecuting rigidity and the polarities inherent in the adversarial conflict. This interaction creates a learning situation which eventually results in stabilizing a mutually satisfactory relationship. This result is usually achieved implicitly, without any explicit intercommunication about the nature of the relationship, its behavioural components or ethical standards.

The relationship will not develop or end quickly if the prosecutor utilizes his power in a highly controlling or arbitrary manner. Under these circumstances the costs of the relationship overbalance the benefits or rewards. The defence counsel's dependence on the reciprocal relationship declines accordingly. At no time must the cost of the relationship outweigh the rewards obtainable by engaging in it. If the same rewards are obtainable outside the relationship there is little benefit in perpetuating it. Direct personal power is rarely exercised in prosecutor-defence relationships. The majority of prosecutors and criminal defence lawyers accept a uniform set of ethics, rules, or norms which act as a set of directives for the interacting members of the environment. As Homans has said: "A norm, then, is an idea in the minds of the members of a group, an idea that can be put in the form of a statement specifying what the members or other men should do, ought to do, are expected to do under given circumstances ..."[18]

A norm is thus a behavioural rule accepted by the members of the

18 G. C. Homans, The Human Group, 123 (1950).

reciprocal relationship; this acceptance obviates the need for the exercise of personal power to maintain the relationship. In this way aggressions or frustrations are avoided, as members of the interaction perceive adjustments as part of the accepted norm rather than the result of an individual's exercise of power.[19] Each member of the group is as aware of behaviour which is acceptable in certain situations as he is of behaviour unacceptable under similar circumstances. No lawyer involved in the reciprocal relationships need be told not to use evidence, given him in confidence by the prosecution, to impeach Crown witnesses. Norms stabilize the available pre-trial negotiating procedures without the need for individual decisions in each case about the procedure to be followed. The acceptance of the norm insures smooth interaction without interference by individual whim or by unexpected shifts in prosecutor or defence behaviour.

5 HIDDEN CONSENSUS

Part of the uneasiness generated by reciprocal relationships is the seemingly patternless decision-making, and the individual capriciousness encouraged by the absence of formal rules and regulated scrutiny of the interaction. Where there is little opportunity for open scrutiny the suspicion is aroused that arbitrary behaviour by individuals with power will critically affect the life and liberty of others. But as Skolnick has suggested: "A lawless unlimited power expressing itself solely in unpredictable and patternless interventions in human affairs could be said to be unjust only in the sense that it does not act by known rule. It would be hard to call it unjust in any more specific sense until one discovered what hidden principle, if any, guided its interventions."[20]

There may exist a continuing high level of conformity to behavioural norms which could be said to represent laws in a functional sense without the usual available authoritative sanction. These habitual modes of interaction are subject neither to commands nor to controls in the conventional sense. Rather than control by a superior or independent authority, the stability of the relationship is preserved by these norms.

19 *Ibid.*, at p. 138.
20 Skolnick, *Justice without Trial*, at p. 15.

They constitute a form of self-regulation within the limitations set by the system. Although seemingly patternless this is in fact, in the majority of pre-trial negotiations, a patterned action based on norms accepted by the majority which permit little individual arbitrary action. This "hidden stratum of consensus"[21] lies beneath the formalized conflict and confrontation of the trial. Co-operative solutions to maximize gains continue below the crust of competitive formalities. They fall within a general patterned system of self-regulation beyond legislative and judicial scrutiny and outside the courtroom.

Despite the habitual or normative forms of conduct which characterize reciprocal relationships within the legal environment there is the important question about the underlying criteria for decision-making within the relationship. Whether these relationships can coexist with the professed goals and ideological commitments of the legal system, or are merely a haphazard growth tied to the demands of a substratum system with little consideration of the long-range ideological consequences, is not clear. As noted, prosecutors rarely question the goals, or even the worthwhileness of it all, as they are primarily occupied in doing what they are doing without adequate opportunity or time to reflect upon the significance of the long-range consequences of their activities. Speculative qualities have little application to the critical contingencies of the here and now. They are not acting randomly but within common definitions of the situation in which they and those with whom they interact find themselves. But there is a distinction between acting to adjust best to currently pressing utilitarian considerations and acting to perpetuate best the goals, ideals, and values of the legal system. Professor Coons, in his discussion of the role of compromise in a judicial setting, has said:

Any judicial system involves continuing accommodation between the need to preserve a coherent set of ordering principles and the quest for tolerable results in individual disputes ... but one test of any system is the incidence of compatibility between dominating formal theory and justice for individual litigants. Constant harmony between the two is an unattainable ideal – but an ideal nonetheless.[22]

21 M. Barkun, *Law without Sanctions*, 39 (1968).
22 See Coons, "Approaches to Court Imposed Compromise," at p. 751.

We do make a distinction between what prosecutors ought to do to conform to the goals of the system and what prosecutors do in fact, between the ideals of the system and its operational conditions. These are not clear distinctions for prosecutors. When they act, they do not do so purely from functional motivations. Acts involve beliefs even though those beliefs may differ from the ones that are asserted by the formal requirements of the legal system. The dichotomy between the ideal and the practice is not so much a disassociation from the ideal as it is an accommodation to competing considerations.[23] The acceptance of any goal depends primarily on the knowledge that there are adequate means available to carry out that goal. Overburdened and understaffed courts encourage the development of instinctive reactions or accommodations to administrative demands. Particularly if the goals are not clearly enunciated and understood by those engaged in implementation it is likely that official standards of conduct will not be maintained. Not only is widespread understanding of the nature of the ends required but there must be co-ordinated action by those who wish to attain these ends. If the means are unavailable to attain the goals or if the goals themselves are not clearly understood or accepted by the majority of those who are called upon to implement them, the dichotomy between the law in theory and the law in fact is necessarily perpetuated.

Among the enunciated ideals of the legal system is the adversarial concept of criminal justice and the courtroom and evidentiary protections inherent in that concept. Conflict is ritualized by procedural formalities and evidentiary restrictions that support the theory that adversarial conflict is the best available method for discovering the truth and for attaining justice for the parties. The gap between these enunciated principles and actual conduct is apparent. The informal adjustments which dominate life itself, that determine the majority of criminal dispositions even though not printed or enunciated as part of any general legal proposition – these are the living law.[24]

---

23 See K. D. Naegele, *Some Observations in the Scope of Sociological Analysis in Theories of Society* (T. Parsons, E. Shils, K. D. Naegele, and J. R. Pitts, eds., 1961).
24 See generally E. Ehrlich, *Fundamental Principles of Sociology of Law* (1936).

Adversarial conflict and its ritualization at trial is incompatible with the more satisfactory conciliatory adjustments which assure more consistent and reliable outcomes. As long as reciprocal relationships and compromise provide more benefits to defence and prosecution than those provided by the trial process, criminal cases will continue to be adjusted outside the courtroom.

CHAPTER NINE

Reappraisal and Reform

1 TRAINING FOR PROSECUTION

Criminal law courses in Canada, as elsewhere, have been the Cinderellas of the law school curriculum. Little more than the basic principles of criminal law and procedure is taught, quite often in the first year, so that on graduation only a hazy concept of the rudimentaries remain. For a law student who intends eventually to specialize in the criminal law the law schools have, until recently, displayed little interest in offering courses to supplement his basic fare in criminal law. At graduation, the law student knows little about criminological or peno-correctional philosophy, nor has he developed an appreciation of the social and ethical values which ought to dominate the administration of criminal justice. By offering more sophisticated criminal law options an attempt should be made to provide insight into correction theories and administrative practices and to heighten sensitivity to human behaviour and pressing social problems.

The young graduates who join the prosecutor's office directly after completion of their law school training lose the opportunity of gaining the variety of perspectives open to those who have engaged in the general practice of law before they enter into the formative atmosphere of the prosecuting environment. No formal pre-prosecutorial training is available to the novice. He is thrust directly into the lowest level of prosecutions, the "impaired driving" court, where he is subjected to a wide range of desensitizing experiences. Although we do not know the extent to which practices in the criminal justice system vary with the levels of competence of the prosecutors, it is highly probable that the more skilled and experienced, the more sensitive and better trained prosecutors become, the more consistent and able will be their performance.

In the future, appointment of prosecutors should not be based, as it is today, solely on successful graduation, but in addition, a minimum of two years in general practice, government service, or criminal defence practice should be considered as an important prerequisite to appointment. After appointment, but before the young prosecutors engage in prosecuting practice, training should be provided in order to develop some self-awareness among them. An understanding of the scope and limits of their new powers as well as the system in which they must work is essential. Such a program may help to stimulate discussions of the criteria on which prosecutorial decision-making is based. Active involvement of the new appointees in group discussions among prosecutors aimed at clarifying the values and attainability of group goals may help to promote their assimilation. As Thibault and Kelley suggest:

As long as group members are interdependent in attaining their goals, there must be wide acceptance of the chosen means as well as of the goals themselves. Indeed, as we have noted before, goal acceptance often hinges upon knowledge that an adequate means is available. Furthermore, the co-ordinated joint action of many members that is necessary to reach certain goals requires widespread understanding of the nature of the chosen means. If general participation in developing and planning a means heightens understanding of it and commitment to it, the group-problem-solving process may be more economical in the long run than one that begins with the most expert thought and advice.[1]

Articulation of goals serves to strengthen legal norms in the face of police and other pre-trial influences. Analysis of the system could provide the young prosecutor with an overview of many stages of the criminal justice system and an appreciation of the means employed to accomplish different ends. Prosecuting practice, no longer seen as self-contained, would be reshaped within its broader operational context. Some accommodation between due process and crime control values is more likely if the conflict between the two is made explicit and the merits of the contrasting commitments analysed. Centrally located

1 See Thibault and Kelley, *The Social Psychology of Groups* (1959), at p. 272.

training, provided for all prospective prosecutors, may represent the most effective method of developing norms and practices which will become uniform across the country.

Guidance should not end at the completion of a six- or eight-week course, but the learning process should be sustained by placing the new appointee, not in the lowest courts in the rough and ready atmosphere that encourages callousness and slipshod preparation of cases, but, instead, in the higher courts where he should be, at least for a short time, apprenticed to a senior prosecutor. Apprenticeship to a skilled senior man would check the early development of bad habits and encourage the careful preparation of argument which is characteristic of the higher courts. Only at the conclusion of his apprenticeship should the novice move to the lower courts where the habits of preparation and argument, gained during his apprenticeship, may assist in uplifting current practices and in sustaining legal norms against distortion encouraged by the demands of the lower court scramble.

2 THE DECISION TO PROSECUTE

Implementation of acceptable legal norms which will eventually dominate the prosecuting processes must commence at the initial stage when the criminal prosecution is invoked. Decisions to initiate criminal prosecution must be based on legal criteria and not on an individual police officer's exercise of his discretion or on police enforcement policy. In order to insure that legal standards control the initiation of the prosecution, an assessor, trained in the law, who would assess all charges and the evidence in support, should be appointed to assist the office of prosecution. Assessors would not themselves engage in prosecution but would act to control and screen criminal cases by the application of legal evidentiary standards to all charges whether initiated by the police or by private complaint. Unnecessary prosecutions based on insufficient evidence and overcharging by police would be sharply curtailed. The need to withdraw or reduce charges at a later stage would be substantially lessened by an effective screening process. The criteria on which prosecutions are to be withdrawn, reduced, or pursued, would be enunciated by the prosecutor's or the Attorney General's office, independent of the encroaching influences of enforcement policy pursued by police. Employment of a full-time legal adviser by the police would replace their present reliance on their own judgment or on a prosecutor's legal advice and direction.

3 CASE RESPONSIBILITY

Reassessment is also required of the current fragmentation of prosecuting assignments, which results in a number of prosecutors handling a particular case as it reaches different courtrooms. Assignment of prosecutors to courtrooms rather than to cases should only be necessary where guilty pleas are entered at the first instance and in summary offences such as impaired driving, traffic, and by-law offences. In the majority of cases one prosecutor should be made responsible for a case, not a particular courtroom. This means that once a plea of not guilty has been entered, one prosecutor assigned to the case should follow it through the pre-trial procedural stages to its ultimate disposition at trial. Currently the practice of case assignment is narrowly limited to those instances which gain public notoriety or those which are particularly complex. Case assignment as a rule rather than an exception would encourage some continuity between the prosecutor and the case, and accordingly improve his ability to make an early assessment of its strengths and weaknesses. Since the quality of his decisions must be based ultimately on the quality of the information available to him, the early acquisition of information and his continual contact with the problems of a particular prosecution would substantially improve the quality of his decisions.

4 THE TAMING OF DISCRETION

Dispositional convenience is based on informality and the wide discretionary power exercised by the prosecution. The use of discretionary power creates a means for the disposition of a large number of criminal cases without trial, challenge, or confrontation. Procedural and evidentiary safeguards are often by-passed in the informal atmosphere of pre-trial dispositions. Criticism of prosecuting practices is founded, in part, on the incompatibility of the exercise of wide powers of discretion with the rule of law. Traditional legal concepts have supported the proposition: "Causes criminal are not arbitrable because they ought to be punished for the common good."[2]

Modification of procedural protections and rule of law standards by police, prosecution, and the defence gives rise to the suspicion that discretion may be used arbitrarily for purposes that are irrelevant to the accused and the charge against him. Conformity to the rule of law requires precise standards for authoritative interference with individual rights and firm procedural safeguards to limit official power. Abasement of the rule of law by the informal exercise of discretion may engender public disrespect and distrust of legal institutions which too often seem subject to administrative manipulation.

It is arguable that the shift away from the rule of law, the adversarial processes and its protections, must be stopped altogether and the rule of law reaffirmed in pre-trial as well as trial procedure.[3] It seems, however, that such a shift would encourage a return to rigidity that would bury the benefits of flexibility along with the threats of discretionary abuse. It is obviously an impossible and undesirable goal to carry out all laws without discretionary interpretation in applying them.[4] Hence the elimination or even the reduction of prosecutorial discretion is not the answer. But the frank recognition of the steady growth of discretion in the administration of criminal law is a first step toward imposing the controls necessary to maintain the protections inherent in the judicially administered adversary system and to avoid the abuses of arbitrary or merely improvised administrative decisions.

The combination of open, yet informal, negotiation with the observance of due process standards may be started by reducing the prosecutors' exclusive control of information and mechanisms which sustain their present private preserves of power. For example, pre-trial disclosure, which can seriously impair the liberty of the accused and the preparation of his defence, should no longer depend upon the quality of the reciprocal relationship between defence and prosecution.

The Council of the Law Society in England recently recommended

2 *Bacon's Abridgment, Arb. A:* "If the offence is of a public nature no agreement can be valid that is founded on the consideration of stifling a prosecution for it." *per* L. J. Denman, in *Keir* v. *Leeman* (1844), 6 Q.B. 308 at p. 321. See also *Baker* v. *Townsend* (1817), 7 Taunt. 422, and generally, F. Russell, *Arbitration,* 5–6 (14th ed., 1949).

3 See *Essays in Criminal Science,* 77, 82 (G. O. W. Mueller, ed., 1961).

4 Brietel, "Controls in Criminal Law Enforcement," 27 *U. of Chi. L. Rev.* 427 (1960).

compulsory pre-trial disclosure by the prosecution and in doing so criticized present practices:

The current practice under which a defending advocate must depend not upon the rights of the accused, but upon the goodwill and benignity of the prosecuting advocate is an inadequate basis for procedures designed to determine a citizen's rights to remain at liberty. Not only is an unrepresented accused or one whose legal adviser is *persona non grata* with a particular prosecutor subject to a substantial disadvantage, but the extent to which any particular prosecutor will reveal the nature of the evidence, even to those defence representatives who are known to and respected by him always remains highly questionable.[5]

Full disclosure of the prosecution's case should be provided to the accused immediately after a charge has been laid. If further disclosure of prosecution witnesses or scientific tests are required, provision should be made for discovery by the defence of the particulars of the case, including the right of the accused to obtain a list of all the prosecution witnesses and their statements.[6] Pre-trial disclosure will not be effective unless each accused is represented by counsel who can, before the trial, competently assess the weight of the prosecution's case and in the light of this assessment, enter into negotiations to safeguard the best interests of the accused.

Similarly, conciliation and compromise of guilty pleas should no longer be subject to the whim of professional courtesies or the inequalities of reciprocal relationships. Pre-trial conciliation leading to the reduction or withdrawal of charges should be made subject to judicial confirmation.[7] Judicial supervision and inquiry will act as a bulwark

5 See Council of the Law Society of England, Memorandum, December 1965.
6 See *Dallison* v. *Caffery*, [1964] 2 All E.R. 610, at 618, where Lord Denning said: "The duty of a prosecuting counsel or solicitor, as I have always understood it, is this: if he knows of a credible witness who can speak to material facts which tend to show the prisoner to be innocent, he must either call that witness himself or make his statement available to the defence. It would be highly reprehensible to conceal from the court evidence which such a witness can give. If the prosecuting counsel or solicitor knows, not of a credible witness, but a witness whom he does not accept as credible, he should tell the defence about him so that they can call him if they wish." See also *Standards Relating to Discovery and Procedure Before Trial*, Am. Bar Assoc. Project on Minimum Standards for Criminal Justice, Tentative Draft (1969).
7 The New York Code of Criminal Procedure, s. 342a, provides: "In any case where the court upon the recommendation of the District Attorney, and in furtherance of justice, accepts a plea of guilty to a crime or offence of a lesser degree or for which a lesser punishment is prescribed than the crime or offence charged, it shall be the duty of the District Attorney to submit to the court

against oppression of the accused and reduce the primacy of administrative expediency in the solution offered. Close control by the judiciary, or another supervising body, over delegated authority and discretionary decisions is crucial to the rights and the dignity of individuals subjected to the administrative processes of criminal justice. This control will better insure that judicial and legal goals will not be thwarted by policies designed to improve administrative efficiency or law enforcement. Controlled compromise will soften the harshness implicit in the over simplified all-or-nothing solution of the adversarial system. It does so by creating an opportunity to choose a variety of solutions better suited to the situation of the individual accused and his eventual rehabilitation.

After the completion of the study a letter was received from an inmate of the Toronto Jail:

Now that it has been admitted that these deals do exist an investigation into their actual results would bring some interesting facts to light. It would show that rather than being for the "benefit of the defendant," they tend to "lead the sheep to the slaughter." I am sure that the crown attorney and the defence lawyer are acting in a conscientious manner, but they tend to promise that which they cannot produce, not having brought the trial judge into their confidence. The perversion of justice comes in when an accused is promised one thing and receives quite another. A point to look into is the fact that quite often a man is charged with a more serious offence, then has it reduced to the offence that he should have been charged with in the first place. He then receives the maximum penalty on the lesser offence. In my opinion the pre-trial deal should be enacted with the concurrence of the trial judge who, after all, is the final arbitrator, or there should be no pre-trial deal at all.

To be sure, judicial scrutiny of pre-trial conciliation in itself offers no panacea, for administrative demands may influence the judiciary as much as the prosecution. It is hoped, however, that in the future judicial supervision and prosecutorial discretion will be exercised within legislative, judicial, or administrative guidelines. These will prescribe in broad terms the consecutive and the alternative processes by which pre-trial negotiations are to be determined. In that event, these processes will no longer be subject to individual caprice but will instead be largely determined by judicial or legislative standards. The duty will be cast clearly upon the judiciary to supervise the "law in action" and

a statement in writing in which his reasons for recommending the acceptance of such plea shall be clearly set forth."

observe the manner in which it functions. If the function is deranged, the judiciary, in accordance with the guidelines, would order adjustments and invoke sanctions to guarantee that behaviour conform with the established standards.

The proposed structure of supervisory controls, utilizing enunciated criteria to judge processes that have been made visible, lessens the likelihood of discriminatory enforcement. At the same time, it provides a means for maintaining options for change and flexibility within acceptable limits. Prosecutorial training before appointment, alteration of initiating procedures, the elimination of pockets of prosecutorial power, the visibility and opportunity for judicial review of pre-trial conduct, and the enunciation of legislatively imposed guidelines for the exercise of prosecutorial discretion will ultimately limit the discriminatory exercise of discretion and the inequalities inherent in present practices. Yet they will also maintain the advantages of the alternatives available outside the adversarial contest that have become such a substantial part of the modern administration of criminal justice.

5 NEW DIRECTIONS

Confusion which obscures the ends pursued by the state on the one hand, and the obvious variety of prosecuting values and modes of implementation on the other, encourage individual views about what are the most desirable ends, and the means to be utilized to achieve them. Any ambiguity relating to the limits of state power is dangerous, for it may result in serious interference with individual liberty and lead to manipulation and cynicism among police and prosecution. Since the system involves a continued manipulation of accused individuals, an interference which may affect their entire lives, there should be some constant idea of what are the ends and limits of that interference.

Within the criminal justice system there are joined together a collection of officials with a variety of procedures for the prosecution of criminal offences. The effectiveness of the system may be measured by how well it performs its function. The ultimate question, however, is what *is* its function? As noted, it may be seen primarily as the efficient and expeditious control of crime by processing the greatest number of guilty persons within the shortest time. Another manifest function is to insure that only those who are proven guilty are convicted, and then only after a fair and careful assessment has been carried out according to enunciated procedures. If there is a conflict between these concepts, is there some room for adjustment towards an optimum level of efficient crime control and due process where the one does not excessively inhibit the other, so that guilty offenders are prosecuted and convicted and yet this is done fairly and without oppressiveness and undue risk of the invasion of the rights of innocent citizens? Or is efficiency fundamentally incompatible with due process?

Some consensus about the ends of criminal justice must be developed before an attempt is made to amend the means – the processes of criminal law. For the selection of alternative processes must be tied to ultimate values in order that each of the various steps in the process is directed towards a common end. Each part of the criminal justice system must be assessed, not as a detached part or as a separate jurisdiction with its own value system of which the other parts take cognizance but little interest, but as interrelated phenomena operating within a total systemic context.

New standards and goals cannot be enunciated in one part of the system while old standards and a variety of goals prevail in others. The total process must be seen as a continuum and no part of it can be reformed without the others if a truly consistent policy is to be followed. Once the difficult work of reaching some agreement on a consistent policy has been accomplished, it may be necessary, if the processes are to be adjusted to accommodate the policy, to vary more than just some of the elements of the institution or the procedural steps by which the criminal prosecution is implemented. It may be necessary to vary altogether the structure, the personnel, the material facilities, and even the environment in which the institution has been functioning in the past.[8]

Criminologists have devoted considerable energy and research to the final stage of the criminal prosecution, the sanctioning or depository stage which takes place after the trial is completed and the finding of guilt has been made. It is on this post-trial stage of the criminal prosecution that the criminological and reformative spotlight has been most often focused. It is believed by those concerned with sentencing,

8 See J. Michael and M. J. Adler, *Crime, Law and Social Science*, 254 (1933), for an excellent synthesis of suggested reforms in the administration of criminal justice.

probation, deterrence, and rehabilitation that, by concentrating effort on the examination and improvement of post-trial processes, recidivism will thereby be minimized. New forms of treatment within and without institutional walls have been attempted in order to inhibit the re-entry into the criminal prosecuting process of those who have completed their contacts with the system.

Doubts have been voiced about the efficacy of the final stages of the criminal prosecution, particularly the lack of uniformity in sentencing and in the inability to reform and rehabilitate offenders within present prison structures. By over-committing the limited research and professional resources available to the post-trial stage the initiating processes of arrest and prosecution have remained poorly understood and their relation to trial and post-trial isolated. By subjecting arrest, interrogation, bail, and prosecutorial discretion to close scrutiny it may be found that many persons currently initiated by the police into the criminal prosecuting process, who are eventually tried, acquitted, or sentenced, may have been otherwise dealt with than through criminal prosecution and that they need not have been made subject to the criminal process at all. Only when the nature of our selective procedures and their operation are clearly understood will we understand who is selected for criminal prosecution and upon what criteria that decision is made. As a result of information gained from such an inquiry, post-trial efforts at rehabilitation and reform may become properly focused.

Illness and victimless forms of anti-social behaviour which are designated as criminal and which do not constitute a threat to public order or safety should be treated by alternative non-criminal procedures and facilities. Drunkenness, minor juvenile drug offences, consensual sexual acts between adults in private, and marital disputes should not be subjected to criminal prosecution thereby overburdening the police, prosecutors and judges with cases better dealt with through non-compulsory treatment provided by social welfare or private agencies. Adjudication in these cases is unnecessary and imprisonment clearly inappropriate, harmful, and destructive of any hope of reintegrating the individual into society as a useful citizen. The restriction of criminal labels to that conduct alone which constitutes a threat to life, property, or public order would help to make available court facilities for the more serious cases and reduce the need for prosecutors to rely on pre-trial negotiation in order to expedite a crowded court calendar.

Proposals for reform cannot be based only on an analysis of one part of the criminal justice system without considering the totality. Similarly, the reform of one system of criminal prosecution should benefit from an analysis of systems in other countries and their success in coping with the crime problem. It is of more than academic interest to compare the broad outline and the divergencies in prosecuting structures in England, France, the United States, and Canada. But a more rewarding exercise is the comparison, not of legislative structures, but of the operational adjustments which necessarily take place within the legislative structure in these countries. It may be found, after careful empirical research, that though the legislative and administrative structures differ substantially from country to country the day-to-day operational realities found in urban, high-crime areas whether in London, New York, Paris, or Toronto have much in common. Before a comparative functional analysis can be performed the operational reality of each system must be probed in order to understand the dimension of the drift from legislative and judicial principles. Do prosecutors in Paris exercise less discretion than those in London? To engage in useful comparative research in this area the investigator must probe beyond legislative categories and procedural labels, beyond the semantics of the respective criminal codes, to examine and compare functions. The consequences of different types of social atmosphere on the administration of criminal justice may be studied more systematically once the atmospheres themselves are functionally described.

Before a rule can be formulated about the behaviour desired, the behaviour itself must be carefully defined, for only then can the legislative policy regarding the conduct that should or should not be required be clearly established. The absence of factual information has, in the past, permitted free reign to informal decisions based on unknown and unofficial policy considerations. Frank exposure of the facts and the criteria on which decisions are based is a prerequisite to any attempt at appraisal or reform. As Thibault and Kelley have suggested:

... the greater the extent to which all the actions of members are open to view, the more thoroughly can surveillance be maintained. If behavior can be practised in privacy, the real impact of the norm may be greatly reduced. This may yield a state of *pluralistic ignorance* in which the common ideas about the amount of conformity to the norm are greatly at variance with the actual facts of conformity.[9]

Once the behaviour has been ascertained, conformity to a stated rule requires surveillance and constant evaluation of the degree to which the behaviour conforms to or deviates from the statutory standard. Any attempt to establish statutory standards or control will be impeded where the interacting groups adhere to their own normative standards by virtue of unarticulated reciprocal covenants and where failure to conform is penalized solely by exclusion from the interaction. In addition to monitoring behaviour, provision must be made for applying sanctions in order to control behaviour inconsistent with the stated rule. In this way conduct would no longer be ordered exclusively by inner groupings or associations within the environment but would also be made to conform to stated institutional goals. Supervision supported by power to impose sanctions would eventually lessen the obvious dichotomy between the stated goals of the legal system and the unarticulated administrative goals. This does not mean that the rules relating to discretion must be imprisoned within the sections of a procedural code, code of ethics, or administrative code of prosecuting practice; nor does it mean that the adversarial system along with all its protections must be imported into the pre-trial processes. Neither procedure would eliminate the exercise of discretion but merely drive it further underground into new channels of expression. What is required is a means to maintain flexibility and arrest arbitrary power.

Visible and monitored flexibility should continue to be encouraged in order to harmonize the rigidity of formulated laws with recognized human values. Legislative overcriminalization of conduct may continue to be corrected by suitable discretionary interpretation. Conciliation and compromise of cases in order to obtain guilty pleas is plainly practical, not only because the sheer volume of cases demands it, but because compromise and conciliation are often more precise procedures with which to handle individual problems than the all-or-nothing solution available in the adversarial forum. Visibility and control may provide a creative method of combining the virtues of flexible conciliation with the traditional goals and standards of the legal system.

9 Thibault and Kelley, *The Social Psychology of Groups*, at p. 246.

Methodology

A / THE SETTING AND SAMPLE

A pilot study was conducted in the autumn of 1966 when fifteen prosecutors out of a total of twenty-two in the city of Montreal were interviewed. Once the data from the pilot study had been analysed and the interviewing technique revised a further pre-test study was commenced in the city of Ottawa. Since Ottawa is a much smaller city than Montreal it seemed likely that procedures, practices, and prosecutor responses might differ from those in the larger city. The prosecutors in the city of Ottawa, five in all, were interviewed over a period of one week. Both these preliminary studies were devoted to the development of interview techniques and an interview schedule. On December 1, 1966, interviews were initiated in Toronto.

B / INTERVIEW TECHNIQUES

Each interview was conducted by the author and lasted from three to six hours. In addition to the interview schedule and the use of probes, problems of response to questions were dealt with by the use of neutral questions such as "How do you mean?"; "I'd like to know more about your thinking on that"; "I'm not sure I understand what you have in mind." The use of probes and neutral questions in addition to the questions developed in the interview schedule eventually led to an interviewing technique whereby the schedule was regarded as a base limiting structure from which the interviewer ranged freely, mindful of the objectives and limits of the study. In this way one response led to another and no rigid sequence of pre-arranged questions was forced upon the interviewee. An attempt was made to cover the questions in the interview schedule but at the same time trying not to force the information into preconceived patterns that might lead to preconceived results.

C / RECORDING THE INTERVIEWS

Accuracy would have been assured if the interviews had been recorded verbatim by the employment of tape-recording devices. The presence of a recording device, it was felt would completely inhibit the subject's response. Extensive notes were taken by the interviewer during the interview. An attempt was made to quote the subject directly. Immediately after the conclusion of the interview it was tape-recorded from notes and memory. The time lapse was minimal between interview and recording. Recording errors often occur because of the interviewer's tendency to round-out, amplify, or otherwise modify responses. Awareness of this problem may have assured some accuracy in the transposition from notes to the tape recording.

The Interview Schedule

A

Explanation of the nature of the research.

Anonymity of the interviewee will be protected.

Age.

Marital status – children.

Education.

What did you do after graduation?

Number of years in practice (if any)?

Were you satisfied with practice before entering the office of the Crown Attorney?

When did you join the office?

What kind of work did you do when you were first appointed? For what period of time? Training process?

What type of work do you do today as an assistant Crown Attorney? What are your responsibilities? How do you spend your day?

Probe salary and attitude toward income.

Probe attitude toward legal education and his own training opportunities.

What are your pastimes or hobbies? Do you participate in public life at all? What are the occupations of your closest friends?

What made you decide to join the office of the Crown Attorney and to become a prosecutor?

B

What are the satisfactions of being a prosecutor? The dissatisfactions?

What are the barriers, if any, to effectively carrying out your function?

Do the police limit your effectiveness? In what way?

Do defence lawyers limit your effectiveness? In what way?

Does the judiciary limit your effectiveness? In what way?

Does legislation limit your effectiveness? In what way?

What is the main function of a prosecutor?

C

What pressures do you have to deal with as an assistant Crown Attorney that a general practitioner or defence lawyer would not normally face? Any political pressures?

Do the communications media, such as the press, influence you or your action in any way?

Must you engage in any public relations functions?

Are there any pressures to produce convictions – by superiors, by the police?

What pressures might the police attempt to exert?

Are there any pressures from the judiciary?

What are the administrative pressures – case load?

How many cases do you normally handle in a week?

What is your contact with each of these cases? How much time do you spend on cases and what factors determine the time spent?

What help or hindrance are the police in the administrative process?

In what types of cases are you consulted by the police before an arrest is made?

Who lays the charge? Are there any controls exercised by prosecutors over the laying of charges?

Are these arrests for purposes other than prosecution?

Once a charge is laid, who drafts the information?

At what point do you first come into contact with the case?

D

In what areas do you exercise your discretion (i.e., charges, initiating prosecution, bail, sentencing)?

What are the factors that influence your decision to oppose bail in a particular case?

How do you find judges react to the Crown's submissions on questions of bail?

Do they follow your submission? If not, why? If they do, why do you think they do?

What are the benefits of having a man in custody pending his trial?

Are there any problems that delay the prompt arraignment of an accused?

Is the present system of bail adequate?

Should defence counsel be present to represent an accused prior to his trial?

Some lawyers suggest that an accused should be advised of a right to counsel when he is first taken into custody by the police. What do you think? At what point in time should he be permitted the advice of a lawyer?

Do you feel that the arrangements for legal aid are adequate?*

E

What type of negotiations might you enter into with defence counsel when an accused wishes to plead guilty to one charge if you will withdraw another?

What are the factors that you might consider before acquiescing in this request?

Would you exercise your own discretion or check with a superior?

Once a charge is laid under what circumstances might you not proceed; under what circumstances might a charge be withdrawn?

Who would make these decisions – to drop one charge and proceed with another, or to accept a plea of guilty to one charge and drop the other(s)?

What factors influence you in making these decisions?

Are there any offences where it is more common to agree to a reduction of a charge if the accused enters a plea of guilty than is the case in others?

*At the time the study was conducted the legal aid system in the province was in the process of a complete revision. As a result, responses to this question have not been reported.

Under what circumstances, if any, when an offence has been committed, would a charge not be laid? Once laid – withdrawn? Once laid – *nolle prosequi*?

Under what circumstances might you agree with defence counsel's submissions to be made on sentence?

F

Are there different types of lawyers that you deal with? What are the differences?

What are your relations like with defence lawyers?

What is your opinion of the quality of the defence lawyers with whom you come into contact?

Are there, in your opinion, different types of defence lawyers? What is your relationship with each type?

If you felt a defence lawyer was a certain type rather than another, would this affect your negotiations (or disclosure) with him?

Do you find there are problems with defence lawyers? What are they? How do you handle them?

G

If you were asked to advise a young lawyer who wished to join the office of the Crown Attorney, what would you tell him are the qualities or characteristics an assistant Crown Attorney should have in order to be successful?

Cases

Index

This book

was designed by

ANTJE LINGNER

under the direction of

ALLAN FLEMING

and was printed by

University of

Toronto

Press